ShiftPoetry™
IN THE TIME OF
COVID-19

An Anthology of Healing Poems
and a Workbook to Help You
Write Yourself Well

EDITED BY

Barbara Ligeti & Howard Kern

ShiftPoetry™ in the Time of COVID-19:
An Anthology of Healing Poems and a Workbook to Help You Write Yourself Well

EDITED BY Barbara Ligeti and Howard Kern

© 2020 by Fifteen Minutes to Shift LLC

All rights reserved. No part of this book may be reproduced in any form or by any electronic or mechanical means, including information storage and retrieval systems, without permission in writing from the publisher, except by a reviewer, who may quote brief passages in a review. For permissions, please write to address below or email barbaraligeti@mac.com. Any members of education institutions wishing to photocopy or electronically reproduce part or all of the work for classroom use, or publishers who would like to obtain permission to include the work in an anthology, should send their inquiries to ShiftPoetry™ c/o Barbara Ligeti, 910 West End Avenue—Suite 6F, New York, NY 10025.

ISBN 978-1-7348787-0-7 (trade paperback original)
ISBN 978-1-7348787-1-4 (Ebook)

First edition published May 2020

BISAC category code
SEL027000: Self-Help/Personal Growth/Success

COVER AND BOOK DESIGN:
KG Design International
www.katgeorges.com
kgeokat@mac.com

Fifteen Minutes to Shift LLC
910 West End Avenue—Suite 6F
New York, NY 10025.
www.ShiftPoetry.com
info@shiftpoetry.com

Dedicated to
doctors, nurses, other health care workers, fire fighters, police officers,
postal workers, people working in necessary service shops,
delivery folks, food preparers, social workers, sanitation workers,
truck drivers, and 911 staff

Also
Governors Gavin Newsom, Andrew Cuomo, and Gretchen Whitmer,
and all other political officials working to end this pandemic.

TABLE OF CONTENTS

Introduction . . . . *i*

How to Use this Book . . . . *iv*

Opening Poem . . . . *vi*

Prompts, Poems, and Workbook *1*

About the Contributors *144*

Acknowledgements *151*

About ShiftPoetry™ *152*

INTRODUCTION

We are living in a time, and in a world, which for most people alive today would have been unthinkable and unknowable a few short months ago, when the calendar flipped to the first day of the third decade of the 21st Century.

We are "self-isolating." We are apart from our friends and loved ones. Alone with our thoughts and at safe social distance from each other. We are all trying to figure out how to cope. COVID-19 has changed everything.

We offer our program of ShiftPoetry™ as one way to help us all come to terms with this new reality. ShiftPoetry™ is an exercise in self-reflection, self-expression, and self-healing. Simply put, this "technology," conceived by Barbara Ligeti and Howard Kern in the back of a bus during a 2018 yoga retreat and tour of Vietnam, is an approach to writing spontaneously in order to free the mind, confront one's emotions, and promote a feeling of personal well-being.

Our 22nd United States Poet Laureate, Tracy K. Smith, has called poetry "writing without rules." We encourage people to express themselves without restraint or formality, in response to specific prompts designed to explore a deeper consciousness, to open the heart, and to leave the ego behind. The result is a "shift" to a better place. Write yourself well - happy, healthy, and whole. Improve your life, one stanza at a time!

In the medical community this work falls under the category of "bibliotherapy," engaging in positive words to stave off unhappiness, depression, and "dis-ease." We believe that ShiftPoetry™ is more pro-active and forward-thinking than other valuable bibliotherapeutic practices like journaling and memoir writing.

ShiftPoetry™ is derived from Howard's own experience writing himself "from dark to light," after suffering great personal losses in a short period of time, including the deaths of two dear friends and his Mom, while at the same time dealing with his own cancer diagnosis.

During our trip to Vietnam, Howard was constantly writing furiously on his smartphone. Knowing he was a lawyer, Barbara wondered why he was spending so much time working while on the retreat. But he wasn't working. He was actually working out his personal concerns through poetic writing. Howard was essentially acting as his own therapist! Barbara was intrigued.

Soon after returning to LA, we attended multiple sessions of a memoir writing class filled with folks wanting to get in touch with their feelings and perhaps get published. The approach was relatively straightforward but nevertheless triggered some deep emotions. Over time we noticed that many of the writers in the group kept focusing on one story. It occurred to us that we could offer a writing experience that opened the door for personal growth.

So, in April of 2018, we hosted our first workshop. The in-person group experience was simple. Barbara would lead a short meditation. Howard would then read prompts he had written, instructing all to "sprint write" in 10-minute intervals to create an emotional snapshot of the thoughts that came up in response. The only rules were to write from the heart and without judgment. Then we would go around the room and have each "ShiftPoet" read their work out loud. The only response from facilitators and other writers was always a simple heartfelt "thank you." Whatever you write is perfect!

In the two years since ShiftPoetry™'s conception, workshops have been staged regularly across the United States, as well in the Far East and Europe. Prompt subjects have ranged from exploring nature to understanding personal relationships. Our prompts address categories from A to Z (or as we like to say, from "Anxiety to Zen").

For the time being, there can be no in-person groups, so we have adapted the ShiftPoetry™ method to the requirements and restrictions of the times. We're encouraging our community to join group sessions via Zoom. ShiftPoetry™ supplies meditation guidance and Howard's prompts. You write alone in ten minute intervals while on Zoom and read your work out loud to the group, followed by a group "thank you." You can also post your work on our website, www.ShiftPoetry.com, to share it with the community and experience the work of others. The writing you generate in ShiftPoetry™ is yours to collect or re-work. ShiftPoetry™ is not really a writing tutorial; rather it is a self-help, personal expression and coping aid. In the absence of direct contact, we have been building a virtual community to help us all understand and heal.

We are aware that sometimes there is no way to convene with others, even without the special circumstances currently prevailing. We have created ShiftPoetry™ in the Time of COVID-19 to introduce you to our technique, but also to specifically address concerns around COVID-19. We view this as the first in a series of books, ultimately applying our method to all manner of life experience. We hope this pandemic will be contained, or better yet, over completely very soon. In the meantime, we are offering this anthology of healing words, plus "do it yourself" workbook all-in-one, to bring ShiftPoetry™ directly into your homes and hearts.

Be well and stay safe.
Barbara Ligeti and Howard Kern
www.ShiftPoetry.com

We were both diagnosed with COVID-19 which took its toll on each of us. We wrote daily ShiftPoems to deal with illness and individual quarantine. We also hosted a handful of Zoom gatherings to offer community to our regular ShiftPoetry™ participants and were inspired to quickly organize this book because we wanted people to have access to our process while all of us are still experiencing some level of isolation. Included here are many of our poems plus those gathered during our Zoom workshops.

Even when the COVID-19 threat has subsided, we hope this workbook will be of continued inspiration and use to you.

HOW TO USE THIS BOOK

Settle in by closing your eyes and breathing deeply until your mind is clear.

Open your eyes and read a prompt.

Don't overthink the prompt.

Set a timer for 10 minutes and begin "sprint writing" on the blank page opposite the prompt. You can also write more on a pad or in a journal. We recommend writing longhand (not on a computer or your phone).

Turn the page to read poems inspired by each prompt. "ShiftPoets" are not necessarily professional or even aspiring writers. We are nurses, gardeners, artists, scientists, military folks, parents, and grandparents. Author bios are available at the end of the book.

If you are writing with a friend or in a self-styled group, consider having one of you read the prompt out loud before you all begin to write.

Write poetically and with abandon.

When you are done, endeavor to read your poem out loud to a friend, colleague or group. If that is not readily possible, consider posting the poem on our website or otherwise sharing it. You are the author and owner of your own writing and thoughts, so you're free to edit, rework or expand your poems in any way you choose.

Advise your "audience" that your desire is to be heard as a path to self-understanding. Reading out loud will allow you to acknowledge your thoughts and words, and then, "let them go." You will be surprised at how much you will be able to see, learn, and free yourself through this process. Your poem should be acknowledged and not critiqued. Those around you should say "thank you" and nothing more.

Our prompts naturally guide one from dark to light, from issue to solution, from a question to an answer, or at least a greater understanding of the question. We hope that everyone will find understanding and love of self and others with this work.

For more about ShiftPoetry™ please visit our website at www.shiftpoetry.com.

Feel free to be in touch as we widen our community of ShiftPoets.

And "thank you" in advance!!

Barbara Ligeti and Howard Kern
www.ShiftPoetry.com

OPENING POEM

This poem is dedicated to Scott Hollander, the brother of Jeffrey Hollander, one of our ShiftPoets and one of my dearest friends for over forty years. Scott passed away from the virus on April 14, 2020, at the age of 57, just as we were about to put this book to bed. I have taken the liberty of writing the following poem in Jeffrey's voice, one that I know well, to help him with his grief.

Howard Kern, April 22, 2020

The Man in the Bed

You're gone now,
Your bed is empty,
Ten years wiped away as the sheets are laundered,
A history gone,
Poof,
A miracle,
Waiting for another person to create a new story.

But our story started long ago,
Two brothers that followed very different paths,
I had my sword to bear,
Being gay was not something I wore with pride back then,
But I rose up and accepted my true self,
I am who I am and I am proud.

Your issues were not so simple,
Emotional issues never are,
We were raised by the same mother and step-father,
But it wasn't the same for us,
I felt nothing but love from them and learned how to love,
I don't know what you felt because we never talked that way,
I just remember being afraid of you,
You were younger but you were out of control,
Sometimes violent,
Always angry.

Do you remember when you broke my nose?
You threw a 2x4 at me,
Maybe I should have ducked,
But I was frozen in that moment,
Shocked by your rage,
It could have been worse,
But it wasn't,
That is a memory of you I experience every day when I look in the mirror,
My crooked nose,
My broken brother.

(continued)

I forgave you for that,
It never even comes up except with certain people that knew both of us,
You did the best you could,
I don't hold anything against you,
MS crippled you before COVID struck the final blow,
We did have some moments together,
When you no longer were threatening I could see you,
It wasn't your fault that you were angry,
It wasn't anybody's fault,
You were who you were,
And before the last bell tolled,
I loved you warts and all.

It's strange that the day you passed the hospital asked me to play God,
They wanted to know whether you should be put on a ventilator,
You had been in bed for 10 years,
Not much of a life,
But people still loved you,
They cared about you,
Even if they didn't come to see you they asked about you,
So when I was asked about pulling the plug and throwing in the towel,
I said "No,"
I didn't even pause,
I thought about the TV that you still watched,
The sparkle in your eyes behind your ravaged body,
The tears that would be shed when your light was extinguished,
And mom,
Poor mom who also passed too soon,
She loved you,
You were her baby,
I searched deep inside my soul,
And she spoke to me,
She told me to do everything I could to save her baby,
And I obeyed,
I would follow mom's wishes,
I would defer to God.

(continued)

Sure enough,
God did step in,
You did not die in that bed,
You died on a gurney,
Too sick to earn more time,
The respirator going to someone with a brighter future,
And as I promised,
When your flame was extinguished,
Tears were shed,
People loved you,
You mattered,
You existed,
And brother,
My tears were shed,
You and I were different,
But we will forever be connected.

I don't know how many times I said it,
But I always thought it,
And I pray that you felt it,

Scott,
My brother,
My friend,
My sometimes tormentor,
I love you,
I love you,
I love you,
Forever more.

© *Howard Kern, April 2020*

ShiftPoetry™
IN THE TIME OF
COVID-19

PROMPT #1

One does not have to be religious to pray. There is an expression that there are no atheists in foxholes. That does not mean that you have to believe in God or follow any particular teachings. You may find strength in the Universe or may just put things out there. Each one of us is a Divine being and has the power to improve the lives of ourselves and others. Think about a prayer or a powerful blessing that you would like to put out there for humanity to help all of us get through COVID-19 and its aftermath.

When you are ready, begin to write poetically, your heartfelt blessing for yourself and others who have been impacted by this virus.

POEMS INSPIRED BY PROMPT #1

A Prayer for 2020

May the skies remain clear and blue
May your family all pull through
May the reverence remain that the heroes now get
Lest we ever forget

May our future leaders have souls
May we learn to cherish the old
May we find solace in silence and look to the stars
Now that we've found who we are

© Kate Connor, April 2020

A Prayer for All Time

Listen up people.
Quarantined-YES
Alone-NO
"Be still and know I'm God."
We are in the midst of IT, but IT doesn't define us
God does.
We are afraid, but fear is not from God.
God is Love.

YES, stillness surrounds us.
No theatre
No sports
No parades
Just an eerie silence on our city streets
Till 7pm
When Love Reigns.

When in one city, the windows fly open,
the cheering begins,
the cowbells ring,
the gratitude pours forth.

So hold thoughts of gratitude,
well wishes
blessings
hope
healing
all fueled with the emotion of Love.

My faith tells me Love is the answer

Listen up people.
I love you.

© *Pat Patterson, April 2020*

PROMPT #2

There have been many TV shows and movies about getting lost on a deserted island. And for most of us, that was as close as we got to being stranded. That all changed with COVID-19. We all are isolated on our little islands. Many of us have too much TP and not enough TLC.

Think about this isolation and think about who you would like to be sharing it with. Maybe you already are with your perfect quarantine. If not, this is your chance to dream.

When you are ready, write poetically about your dream quarantine mate.

POEMS INSPIRED BY PROMPT #2

Him

Him,
I don't know who he is,
Elusive and Mystical.
Beautiful inside and out.
I love my friends but if I am truly honest I want him.
He is my person,
The one I cuddle up to,
The one who holds me when I cry and I hold him.
It's the only thing I have always wanted that has always eluded me.
And if we are on a desert island or locked up because of a pandemic,
We would make it work,
He is kind and gentle,
Smart and funny,
Confident but humble.

Him,
He is my quarantine confidant,
My Corona Cutie
The ultimate vaccine for isolation,
But like the solution to this pandemic,
He exists somewhere in my future,
And as I share my space with my lovely roommates,
He is what keeps me going,
Knowing that when COVID-19 is a distant memory,
He will fill my future,
And be that man and that boy I crave so much.

Him,
Is it just a fantasy?
The longer I write the further away I feel,
Out in the real world it seems so far away but on my fantasy island,
It's just him and me,
We share stories,
We play,
He's very handy and I'm a great helper.
I entertain and he laughs and smiles,
We dance and I sing to him,
There is plenty of fruit on the island,
No snake to lead us astray,
Just two Adams enjoying our Eden,
Like nectar from heaven,

(continued)

We stay fed and happy for a lifetime together,
No jealousy,
Just Love,
And though I do not know where he is,
I know where to start,
"Alexa, find him,"
A boy can dream . . . Him.

© *Jesse Pudles, April 2020*

Sheltering With Friends

If I could turn back the clock,
I would be sheltering with my best friend Steven and his wife Elissa,
In their home across from the lake.

Normalcy,
History,
Safety,
Laughter,
A solid foundation.

Shared Fears and shared hopes.

We had talked about having me stay with them if things got bad.

But . . . that was just talk,
That was a plan that we never,
In our wildest imagination,
Thought would come to fruition.

And, when,
in a Twilight Zone way,
it did,
it was already too late.

© *Jeffrey Hollander, April 2020*

PROMPT #3

The coronavirus has given all of us a lot more time to be by ourselves. Schools are closed. Offices are closed. One of the only things we are left with is our thoughts. This is an amazing gift. Instead of thinking about what you are missing, think about potential opportunities. Think about what you can do now that you have time. It doesn't have to be epic. It only should be loving.

When you are ready, begin to write poetically what you may do while the world is in a panic.

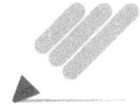

POEMS INSPIRED BY PROMPT #3

My Isolation Fix . . .
In the Time of Corona

I am looking at life in the rear
and just wondering how I got here
this suggestion or question
just sparks indigestion . . .
and no one can answer
I fear

I know that I want to stay sane
and I'm trying hard not to complain
but I'm locked up inside and I think that this ride
may just take till the end of the year

So in order to cope
(no, it's not smoking dope)
I take something to keep
from unhinging
it's a way easy way
just to get through each day
the solution?
It's chocolate binging

All those emails that come
at a staggering sum
make me feel I could drown my computer
but then as I delete
I just sit there and eat
And that chocolate high
makes me neuter

I'm just freaked at the news
and I know I can choose
not to watch anything that's upsetting
but with three bars or so
I can give it a go
and not freak at the info I'm getting

So the thing that's divine, is to get bars online
but make sure that they're medium dark
and just eat maybe four
till you don't care no more
that you may never walk near
a human . . . again.

© *Cynthia Adler, April 2020*

Walking, Walking, Walking.

7–10–12 miles a day.
Exercise has always been one of my gods, but this quarantine has put it on steroids.

Yet each day another path is blocked.
Closed roads
Closed parks
Closed walkways on the Hudson.

Yet, I walk.
Finding a new street, a new adventure.
And in the walking discovering a world I never saw.
Reveling in each discovery.

Whizzing up a hill is not the same as trudging up.
Look at that quaint school
Or the USN Comfort peeking between the 2 beams of the World Trade Center Tribute
A memorial for 5 brothers killed on the USN Juneau in WWII
Parakeet nests
An attacking goose protecting her newborn brood
Almost always there yet not prominent, now a part of my new reality to be
Appreciated
Embraced
Celebrated.

Will I miss my walk?
Seek out the unknown,
Relish the discoveries
or will I put my blinders back on once a more open life returns?

© Pat Patterson, April 2020

PROMPT #4

We all have had conversations with loved ones that maybe we would have done differently if we had been given more time. And even though we know that we said things we did not mean, our egos prevent us from sharing our true feelings. Think about a conversation you had recently or in the past that you would like to do over.

When you are ready, begin to write poetically to that person about your true feelings, keeping your ego at bay. Accepting our humanity is the first step to recovery.

POEMS INSPIRED BY PROMPT #4

Greg's Poem

We are not really in conflict,
You are in conflict with me,
About a simple misunderstanding.

An apology came from me,
Thorough and immediate.

An unedited apology text,
As soon as I realized it,
As soon as the words came to me.

I'm sorry I misunderstood your compliment,
An insulting one in fact.

You never valued yourself before,
That changed.

How?

I heard,
You don't value yourself.

Why?

I assumed we could easily get past it.

Icy silence instead.

Before I forgive you,
I just have to say,
Every guy you ever warned me against,
Was nicer to me,
Than you are right now.

Funny,
Ridiculous
True.

You are doing the best you can.

It's pretty lame.

(continued)

No reason for me to be mad.
I never really was,
Just digesting it.

Writing this will help.

I love you.

© Phoebe Diftler, April 2020

POEMS INSPIRED BY PROMPT #4

Love is not a Preference
For Brock

You're not dead yet,
Joe Average,
But I kind of killed you back there in Hell's Kitchen.
Or us, was it?
The weekend of my wedding,
And the weed at the border.
I have your drawings,
Your paintings and your prints,
I have the heart you gave me.
You showed me how to find you,
You encouraged me,
The way you lived showed me how to live,
How to make art,
How to love not fancy,
But practical and tough you were
a slave to beauty and
A supplicant to truth but
You are not gone yet, Joe,
The end cannot be far, and I dread your passing.

Your last breath will break me because I likely won't have told you that I love you.
Maybe even like that.
I see the errors of my ways,
Back in Hell's Kitchen all I knew was that I didn't love her and that I wasn't gay.
Now I'm learning that love is not a preference.

So I guess I'm saying thank you for saving me.
I'm sorry for not making a life together with you because I was "straight."
Thanks for loving like you do
For living like you do.

I'll wager you'll go out like a lion of love.
And I'll keep making art,
Love, Life and food,
With love in my heart,
Mostly because of the lessons you taught me,
Because of who you are to me,

(continued)

Joe Average,
Nee Brock David Tebbutt
An exceptional person,
A once in a century guy
It's not about gender or sexual attraction,
It's about souls meeting,
And though our bodies never merged,
Your soul will forever dance in my heart.

© Mark Schulte, March 2020

PROMPT #5

I had never been locked away until the Coronavirus. Now I know what it must be like to be in prison or at sea. I am a wanderer and always appreciate the freedom of stepping outside my door and just wandering. I appreciate that even more now that I don't have that freedom.

I have been dealing with illness for close to two weeks. But even without illness, I still am locked up by government order. What is it like for you to be locked up? What do you miss the most from your life pre-Pandemic?

When you are ready, begin to write poetically about what you will do once the world returns to normal. Who will you call? Where will you go?

POEMS INSPIRED BY PROMPT #5

On Isolation and Separation

She's self-isolating.
Just found out she's positive.
Will she slow down?
She's in LA.
No way to touch. To comfort
Can only talk on Skype
Yikes!!
So much for the glamour of a bi-coastal life

Grandkids in Connecticut
Hard to connect with.
No games
No puzzles
No high fives
Can't see the little one crawl
That's the hardest thing of all.
Wonder what they'll remember when it's over . . .

Alone in New York
Growing a beard
Why not?
Maybe I'll clean the apartment.
I really should.
Or fix the hole in wall where the picture fell down
Maybe next week.

Alone, but still, in some ways, closer
More time to talk
More time to think
More time to feel
More time to drink

© *Jeffrey Altshuler, April 2020*

One More Hug

Dear Mom,
You see me delivering food,
But I'm wearing a mask and gloves.

I can't come to your bedside,
So I'm standing at your bedroom door,
Trying to keep COVID at bay.

You may not understand that,
You're extremely unhealthy and considered at risk.
I understand this and my role is now your parent.

You may not remember there's a COVID pandemic,
I feel sad when you don't remember,
And my acceptance wills me to repeat myself without frustration.

Whether you don't understand or don't remember,
The reason doesn't matter.
What matters is I can't come to your bedside,
And give you a hug.

You've said you want to die,
So you don't suffer more pain.
I'm now saying I want you to live,
Until I can give you one more hug.

You see me standing at your bedroom door;
Wearing a mask and gloves,
And praying to keep COVID at bay.
I'm hoping to keep COVID at bay,
So I can hug you one more time.

© Michelle Schrupp, April 2020

PROMPT #6

We are living in turbulent times. Many people are panicking. You may feel like you have no control over your life. That's okay. Most of the time things happen regardless of our best intentions. Free yourself of worry.

Focus on the positive things in your life. Rain is inevitable, but so is sunshine. Let the sun shine in. Release the doom and gloom and treat yourself to the positive. It's all real.

When you are ready, start writing about the positive things in your life. No virus can take everything away from you.

POEMS INSPIRED BY PROMPT #6

COVID-19 Cannot Shake Happy

I miss the touch of little bodies hanging on me,
Saying
"Hold me! Hold me!"
Me explaining,
"I can't, you're getting too big,"
As I lean to pick him/her up to carry down the block.

But . . . am I the only one?
I'm sorta loving this.
Last night I listened to my husband serenade me with the ukulele he hasn't touched in months.
I set the table—
We ate in the dining room this evening.

"Ohhh!!" he said, "we're eating at the big table tonight! Cloth napkins and everything! This looks really nice, love!"

I looked over at my dining partner,
Wearing a horrible tee shirt he loves,
Which he would never sport beyond the back garden.
Shorts which also are only worn in front of me.
Stubbly beard.

I answer,
"Yeah and if you want anything else that sometimes follows dinner . . . like a little dessert . . . there better be some shaving going on. That stuff is very scratchy!"

Presto!!!

I hear water running and the sound of shaving happening.

Funny,
There is absolutely no one I'd rather be with,
We're supposed to be on holiday together in Thailand,
I'm pretending we are!

We are so very lucky!

(continued)

I actually said loudly in Gelson's,
"Look people, just the fact that you're shopping here, well we need to shut up about what isn't here, what we don't have. We're privileged- do you realize how many people can't get anything or don't have the money."

I'm happy to be getting old enough that people just look at my behavior as the rantings of an old lady.

I'm really enjoying being in a relationship that's already 25 years of marriage.

It's all so good.

We have toilet paper (quite by accident).
I'm dancing in the kitchen,
I'm having virtual cocktail parties,
I'm making my husband learn to two-step for a wedding,
Which may or may not occur.

Life is going on!

COVID-19 cannot shake happy.

Just isn't going to happen!

© *Deborah Williams, March 2020*

POEMS INSPIRED BY PROMPT #6

Lemonade

A deepening of long-standing friendships.
Bonds made even stronger.

A feeling of "being there" while painfully alone.

A realization that all of the trivial issues that seemed to occupy my life are,
Now, utterly meaningless.

Health, the actual survival of myself, my family, and my friends, are all that truly matter.

A hope that the world realizes this as well.

Heroes, who just yesterday, were ordinary people.

The sun on my face.

Smiles and hellos from neighbors who never did before.

Mindless Netflix series.

© Jeffrey Hollander, April 2020

Light in Total Darkness

For Sue, who makes really good cookies.

It could be the chocolate chip cookies
But it's hard to find what's good in life today,
Forty thousand deaths in the USA, and counting,
Way more in the world:
Those dead are with me at night.
What's positive about this, he wants to know,
I'm positive about this . . .

The river smells like a river again,
And the air smells like air,
I walk along the estuary at sunset,
The Hudson and the tide running out,
Alone along the water.
It's strange,
People are kinder now from six feet away than they ever were up close.

What doesn't kill you hurts like a mother,
(Truckers bringing baking supplies are essential workers)
Tear jerkers on netflix,
Where'd everybody's chill go?

The hills that microbiologists climb were always germ-laden,
Our new truth is old hat to science,
Perhaps during this lonely pause,
We get to enjoy what's always been there,
Birds filling the hungry silence,
Raccoons rattling trash cans farther and farther from the park.

It's not all spiritual,
Some of it is just nice,
Parking spaces in my neighborhood,
Plural and open for more than three second's time.

To think, to breathe, to be grateful,
To well up in tears,
And most of all,
For Markle Sparkle of the past,
Thank you for reminding me of how much I love chocolate chip cookies.

© Mark Schulte, April 2020

PROMPT #7

Do you remember a time in your life when you were scared? Perhaps it was for a moment. Maybe it has been your entire lifetime. Regardless you have survived and at times even prospered.

When you are afraid, it is easy to go to a dark place. However there are always light cubbyholes to be found. Think about those light places in your life.

Treat yourself to a big slice of happy pie. Let's put away our fears for the moment and write poetically the positive that exists even in the darkest moments. Humans have survived incredible hardship. We will survive Coronavirus and hopefully will open our hearts to the joy of just being.

POEMS INSPIRED BY PROMPT #7

Passover Poem

On the morning of Passover evening
I found out that my friend Y is alive
And off the ventilator! He has survived
The Virus, he has come back from the
Edge of his mortality, from the very brink
Of death, and he has returned to us, the
Living. It is one of those moments when
I find myself searching for words, and
None of them seem sufficient. I feel
Such an overwhelming gratitude to
The universe and to the doctors and
Health workers who guided him on his
Journey, who put their lives on the line
So they could save his. I even feel
Grateful to the Angel of Death for
Passing over him, for sparing my friend,
Even as I feel grief for so many others
Whose loved ones have died, who were
Not so fortunate, whose hopes have ended.

The truth is, I could not imagine my friend
Dying, nor could I imagine my life without

Him being a part of it. We have created
Things together—plays and films—he
Was supposed to be directing a film that
I've written (with his help) this month.
On the night he fell ill, he was recording
A song about the Virus that he had written,
He stayed up all night to make sure that he
Got it right. And then, when he woke up in

The morning, he couldn't breathe well,
His lungs wouldn't work. And the sense of
Danger this gave me made it hard for me to
Breathe too, I could take only shallow half-
Breaths. I just could not imagine how I
Would ever fill the hole that his death would
Leave in my life. And now I don't have to.

(continued)

I know that so many people have died, I
Know that so many have left behind unfillable
Holes in the lives of the people who loved
Them, and who they have loved. If I was a
Better person, I would be weeping now for
All of them, for all they have lost, instead of
Weeping tears of joy for my friend's survival.

But I am not that better person. I'm not.
I just feel such overwhelming gratitude
Right now, to all the doctors and health
Workers who sacrificed so much so that
My friend and others could still live, even to
The Angel of Death again for seeing the blood
On the door, the blood of love and friend-
Ship that all his loved ones had placed there,
And passing him over this time, letting him
Come back to us.

This time of the Virus is terrible, there is
Nothing to give thanks for in what it has
Taken away. And yet I feel so thankful
Right now, I can't help it. And I look
Forward to hearing what my friend Y
Will have to say about his sojourn in
The land of the Dying. Because that's
What it means to beat death, at least for
The moment. We tell each other stories
About what it signifies, being alive.

© *Steve Fife, April 2020*

POEMS INSPIRED BY PROMPT #7

We've Got This

4:30 am
Alexa STOP alarm.
Eyes open, NYC skyline in view
7 deep breaths
"I love you, I'm sorry, please forgive me, thank you"
Thank you God for loving me.
FEET HIT THE FLOOR

Morning coffee, mandatory-necessary-after bourbon, a gift from the gods.

A litany of gratitude that always includes:
"Thank you for my faith"
"Thank you for my grandsons"
"Thank you for my children"
"Thank you for my talent"

Offering up to the light those whom I've told I'd remember in prayer—I do.

Yet this faith makes me suspect, to the intellectuals, the artist, my peers.
OH WELL.

Our relationship hasn't always been this tight.
But as the saying goes "If God seems distant, who moved."
I have
The affair
The anger
The lies
The gossip.

But as I always remind God, my old friend. "Don't forget, you made me. So, you're as much to blame as I am."

Just like a computer about to shut down due to overload, we have been given a reset.

Look at all the good we are experiencing during this isolation.
Parents playing charades in the park
People writing and mailing actual letters
Clear blue skies
Birds chirping
Pollution reduced.

(continued)

So, God, my old friend, thank you for this time and watch over all those who are sick and my son—a nurse.

I know you've got this.
So, I know I do too!

© *Pat Patterson, April 2020*

PROMPT #8

We are living in difficult times. The control that we believed we had has eluded us. When science fails, we can either roll up in a ball or we can call upon a greater power. Each one of us has a divine spark. Take this moment to call upon your inner power and provide yourself with the comfort that you deserve.

When you are ready, begin to write poetically about how everything will be alright.

POEMS INSPIRED BY PROMPT #8

Love in the Time of COVID

No, it's not perfect, not even close, but
it's feathered and warm in my heart, like
roots in my toes, like a flowering spine,
even
if the bark of our tree has been
scarred by repeated hatchet marks,
deep scars that only a lifetime of
love can heal.

But it is in there, in the
heart of love that we find
comfort. What walls have we built
around it? What grappling hooks have we
dug into the mortar of jagged parapets, turning
it to dust by the
merciless dig of steel talons?

Here, within these walls, is where
this wall comes down, where
the healing can begin, in this
quarantine of Lenten sacrifice,
forty days of Lenten sacrifice, that
somehow has the power to purify, to
heal and make whole.

Is it because we were forced to
decide we want peace
once and for all? Because
at war with each other we were
really at war with ourselves, that it wasn't
walls we needed but
silky glassine sheaths,
translucent, permeable, viral, to
infect each other with forgiveness.

(continued)

Perhaps
we were tired of being
hard oak against a storm,
unbending, unyielding. This
time has made us pliable grass,
braiding in the wind and storm,
nourished by the rain.
We lost the battle to win the war.

No, not perfect, not even close, but
an opening door, a drawn bridge.
Open, when
time is not quite properly enclosed;
long blears and smears of
oily time we are learning to
navigate together.

No, not perfect, not even close, but
knitting, somehow, has become a
good pastime.

© Michelle Koza, April 2020

POEMS INSPIRED BY PROMPT #8

The Immortal

I have faced life threatening situations my whole life,
Falling asleep at the wheel on the freeway,
Only to be awakened by a wall of snow,
Going down for two counts in a whirlpool,
Finally putting my feet down to find that it was only three feet deep,
Losing three pints of blood because of a bleeding ulcer,
Returning to the hospital not satisfied that I only had an upset stomach,
Avoiding a transfusion in Cape Cod during the inception of the AIDS epidemic,
Not one but two major motorcycle accidents,
Cancer and a prostatectomy,
Cancer again followed by faith in the Universe,
Finally COVID-19,
Yes,
I survived COVID-19,
The Universe was kind to me,
I didn't even find out I had it until after I was fully recovered,
Some would say that I have a dark cloud overhead,
But they are missing the sun that keeps shining through,
I lost my temper the other day,
I said some things to my younger brother that were cruel,
They were honest,
But they were said in anger,
No disease is going to take me down,
But hate can devour my soul,
I am a work in process,
I still have a long way to go,
But I know that no disease will take me down,
One day I will breathe my last breath,
I will share my last hug,
But it will not be a sad day,
It will be a day that the Universe will say "it's time,"
I may be fallen by a disease,
Or perhaps a tree in the forest,
Or maybe I just won't wake up,
But whenever it happens,
I hope that there is nothing but love in my wake,
If I have said anything hurtful to anyone,
Sorry.

© *Howard Kern, April 2020*

Be Careful What You Wish For

I've been saying this all day—
All week—
Since we all found out really . . .

Americans are so Insulated
So spoiled: Our country's motto has always been
"It Can't Happen Here."

Well, guess what? It did.
It did and it is and it's here
And it's now.

And all I know is what I've always known—
You can't control the circumstances;
Only your response to them.

The good news is
Worrying and not worrying have identical outcomes—
So Chill The F Out already.

What's real?
I'm safe.
I have food and water and cell phone and internet and cats.

I'm Fine.

I'm healthy and I'm Fine.

And really, isn't this the very fantasy scenario I've longed for?

Here's about a month—
Learn a language,
Take YouTube clarinet lessons,
Hang all that artwork—
Hey how about finishing those socks you started knitting three years ago?

I tell you one thing:
I'm going to be angry with myself if
When this is over
(and it WILL be over)
I did nothing to improve myself and my fellow humans.

This is an incredible opportunity to make real change.
I'm committed to this as wholly positive.

(and really, wasn't the whole pre-COVID thing a colossal shitshow anyway?)

What could be more exciting?

© *Ruth Waytz, March 2020*

PROMPT #9

I like to think of movies to describe different times of my life. Sometimes the movies are romantic comedies. Other times they may be dramas. Most of the time I think of my life as a sitcom. What genre best describes your life? Even in horror movies, there are heroes and heroines.

In life we oftentimes cannot control the direction. When times are good, we believe that all is according to plan. However, when times are bad, we feel out of control. The truth is that we always have the same amount of control. But in ShiftPoetry™, we all can direct the action the way we want it to go.

When you are ready, forget your troubles and write your story the way you would like it to be. Maybe part of it is already being filmed, just needs your heart and your imagination to fill in the blanks. The movie has been cast and you are the star.

POEMS INSPIRED BY PROMPT #9

Finding Truth on a Movie Set

I was in the process of a move,
The movers were tending to the framed photos on my bookshelf.

"Are those movie stars?" one of them asked me.

A gush of tender affection wafted through me,
"No," I replied, "they are my adopted parents."

We had adopted one another,
They were childless and what was missing from my biological parents,
I found in them.

Visits to their home,
The one in the picture,
Were like going to a museum,
Every room was appointed with curatorial precision.
Meals were the unveiling of a work of art,
The entertaining of guests took the elaborate orchestration and planning of a gala event.

Initially,
I wondered if this was OCD run amok.

Over time,
I learned that it was a celebration and an expression of gratitude,
They were cherishing the abundance after being forced to survive the second World War in Europe where they went for years without.

Now,
I know how to live my life once we have this pandemic behind us: as if we were on a movie set.

© *Aseem Giri, March 2020*

The Corona Express

We're all on the train
The Hitchcock train
We're all part of the mystery
We're all united by fear
Cary Grant and Eva Marie Saint
In North by Northwest
Martin Landau and James Mason
And all the nameless people like me
Who fill out the supporting cast
We're all in our separate compartments
On the Hitchcock train
And the train has entered a tunnel.
It's dark outside right now
It feels very dark
And there's a little bug in the train
A little tiny bug
And everyone is scared shitless
Hiding in our separate compartments
In our minds we can hear the wings
Of the bug as it flies through the corridors
We are all washing our hands in those tiny
Sinks they have on trains

Because the bug feeds off our dirt
I haven't washed my hands this much
Since I was in kindergarten
We all need to see sunlight again
We all crave the sunlight on the
Other side of the dark tunnel
And we don't know where we're going
Where are we going
I really don't know where we're going

(Are we going North by Northwest?
Those of us in the supporting cast
Are sure that the stars have been told
Leaving us, as usual, here in the dark)

POEMS INSPIRED BY PROMPT #9

(continued)

When we emerge from the tunnel
Will we see the same landscape
That we saw before or will it be
Different? I think it will be or
At least we will see it differently
Our time in the tunnel is not a hiatus
It is part of the journey, our journey
On the Mystery Train
We may not all be Cary Grant or Eva Marie
We may not all be James Mason or Martin Landau
But all of us have the same dream
Dreaming in our separate compartments
Of the time that we emerge into a new world
Of the time we can emerge from our compartments
And hold hands again
Raise hands together again

No longer afraid of bugs
Or each other
Or the dirt on our hands
The dirt than can't be removed
No matter how hard we scrub
The dirt that is as much a part of ourselves
As this dream of joining together
Will it happen, will we get there
Will we see this dream become real
Right now I'm not sure what to think or feel
I hope I will be there and so will you
I hope to be united by something other than fear
With Cary Grant and Eva Marie and Landau
And James Mason and yes, Hitchcock too

© *Steve Fife, March 2020*

I Long to Live in a 50's Sitcom

My parents died back to back, back East
I sought refuge and unconditional love
From the only family I had left
In Mar Vista, a sleepy part of Los Angeles
Where I found a corny cottage
On a treelined street
Across the way from my daughter and her
Modern version of the Brady Bunch
Who wake at dawn and are sound asleep by 8pm
A different life than my mad fast lane existence in New York City
Retrieving my morning paper I can
Squint and see June Cleaver waving "the Beaver"
Off to school
Donna and her hubby Dr. Stone speaking softly in front of their house
About the tragedy of having to fire a clumsy housekeeper
I struggle to adjust
Then COVID-19 descends
There is no one on the streets
The neighborhood costume department struggles
To find enough face masks
To protect anyone brave enough to venture outside
Children crying and confused
Forced to go to school by sitting in front of their computers
Longing instead to whisper in the ears of their friends
I have the virus
I'm isolated
Me longing to someday again hug and break bread
With the Brady Bunch only 50 yards away from me
But for now in another world.
I close my eyes and am hugging and giggling with my girlfriends
As we watch Ricky Nelson become a teenage heartthrob
Instead I am living in his "Lonesome Town"
And my mask hides "a heart full of tears"
As I survive and I will, I will celebrate my new found innocence
For now I think I'll sneak outside and hug a tree

© Barbara Ligeti, March 2020

PROMPT #10

I have the Coronavirus blues. This follows on the heels of three years of a much divided nation. I am tired of being sad. I am tired of being alone. Imagine a time when you truly were happy and were not overwhelmed by the world's problems. Think about how good it feels to be happy.

When you are ready, begin to write about what still brings you happiness even in this post-Apocalyptic age. One day life will be simpler. Think about how beautiful life will be in the post-Donald World.

POEMS INSPIRED BY PROMPT #10

Coronavirus Upside Down

So natural
Gentle hugs of days past
Laughter, hands touching, connecting
Before you arrived.
Your presence unwanted spreading fear, distance
Death.
Social distance
Physical distance, death without dignity
No hand in mine
Only the chilly spikes of an indiscriminate virus.
But,
I do not mind your presence, I respect it
For you Coronavirus, deadly poison stealing lives
Have done something else
By bringing us together
Not God, Allah, ministers, gurus or Jesus
Bringing so many together through bleak remoteness
Alone we glimpse at grief, truth, meaning.
Kindness among neighbors, who before
Your grand appearance never spoke
Strangers brought together through invisibility.
In your desire
To tear apart you've done the unimaginable
Giving us community, connection
Love.

© Stefanie Fletcher, April 2020

My Ancestors Paved the Way

I am Jewish,
I come from a long history of hatred and discrimination,
My lineage has survived the Diaspora and pogroms,
The ovens were littered with the bones of my family,
But somehow my parents and grandparents survived,
The biggest challenge to Jewry pre-Coronavirus was assimilation,
It was getting too comfortable to be "American,"
America follows the New Testament,
It applauds the people that have killed my ancestors,
And now it has a King who openly calls Jews killers,
Who opens the White House to White Supremacists,
I do not know whether there is a God or many,
It doesn't matter,
My time on this earth is limited,
Every day I get one day closer to checking out,
I have survived everything so far,
I am a Jew,
Today I am an American,
But yesterday my ancestors were Georgians and Poles,
Hungarians and Austrians,
Who knows who they were before that,
None of that matters,
The only common thread is that they were all human,
Maybe a false assumption,
So what,
Death has lined my track,
Dogma has led to bloodshed,
My lineage has survived pandemics,
It has survived ruthless leaders,
And I too will survive,
I will one day workout in a room filled with sweaty bodies,
I will run races,
Take walks on the beach,
I will smile because I can,
Politicians come and go,
Long after Trump takes his last breath,
The sun will continue to shine,
Life is not just about sunshine and spring flowers,
We need the rain,
We need the fire to clear the forests,
It ain't always easy,
But what is?

© Howard Kern, March 2020

PROMPT #11

I have felt near death at different times in my life. However, I have never died because I have never been truly ready. I am not going to take life for granted anymore and know that one day the world will continue without me. However, I will be ready and I will have a conversation prepared for the people I hope to encounter on the other side.

Who would you like to have meet you at the Gate? What would you like to say? Let that person or those people know how much you missed them. Today it is just a drill. But someday you may want to thank me for helping you write these words.

Be open and loving in your own words to those that have preceded you to the final destination. Let your heart lead and your mind rest in peace.

POEMS INSPIRED BY PROMPT #11

Hi Grandma

It's been over a quarter of a century,
You were my biggest fan,
You gave me permission to eat as many ice cream sandwiches as I wanted to,
You made me pastina just the way I liked it,
You prepared mayonnaise eggs,
Which I later learned is egg salad,
You always believed in me,
You taught me the Shema,
Which I still recite when I am feeling overwhelmed,
You helped me to believe in myself when there was no reason to do so,
You allowed me to love and be loved,
You gave me the courage to try things that scared the shit out of me,
Sometimes I failed,
And when you were alive,
You still loved me,
I do not know what my life would have been like without you,
You were so brave and loving,
You were more prepared for anything just by reaching into your bra than any boy scout I ever met,
You were my rock,
My everything,
And though you may be gone,
You are not forgotten,
I am me because of you,
You lit up my life with your dentured smile,
When you visited,
Anything was possible,
Thank you for loving me,
And helping me to learn how to love myself.

© *Howard Kern, March 2020*

None of Us Is Immune

It is the year 2020.
The start of a new decade, but so far
It has been the start of a new anxiety,
And the loss of everything that made us feel safe.

11 years ago I was in a car crash that totaled my car
And should have killed me. But it didn't.
In fact I emerged without a scratch. Not one drop of blood.

I emerged from that shattered vehicle with a sense of
Well-being unlike anything I'd felt before. I felt a new
Sense of purpose that has only gotten stronger
Over the years. I have had many crises since then,
Many difficult moments, but I never lost that sense of
Well-being. I never lost that feeling that I would get
Through it. I never lost that strong sense of purpose.

But now I don't know.
But now I feel challenged.
But now I feel vulnerable to whatever is out there.
I feel like all of us are vulnerable now, in a way
That I didn't before, in a way

That we didn't seem to be.

In truth, though, we could die at any time.
All of us. Any of us. Could die. At any time.
Maybe that is a lesson that we need to re-learn,
To become more conscious of how evanescent
Our lives are, how easily our lifelines can be
Snipped at any moment. And then all our
Complicated ventures, all our
Plans, will come to nothing.

What happens at these times of peril
Is that fear takes over. Naked fear.
Our primal fear of self-extinction.
And yet, when you get outside of that fear,
There is beauty in the quiet, there is
A recognition of how much we mean to each other.

POEMS INSPIRED BY PROMPT #11

(continued)

I pray for the strength to stay inside of myself and
Not give way to that panic.
The Unknown is always scary, there's no
Getting around it.

And seeing society collapse into itself, collapse
All around us, is even scarier.

Let us hold hands in our minds
Let us link our thoughts
And raise our voices in a loud hum
That will help us all
Find a path out of this dark forest
Into the sunlight again.
The clean, beautiful sunlight
That is still out there, not too far away.
That is still out there, and always will be.

That's what I'm hoping for anyway.
For all of us. For you and for me.

© *Steve Fife, March 2020*

Maximus

This life time of yours
Only two in dog stars
Stumbling through hospital doors
Or out the back of a car

You never complained
About your lot in life
Or the long standing pain
When it cut like a knife

Your tail didn't wag
And your legs were so weak
But your smile never sagged
When you strut on the street

(continued)

It seems you don't know
The long road that you towed
You just go with the flow
No debts do you owe

Your eyes they are kind
Your face is dark black
And always bear in mind
Your love for that snack

The future was uncertain
As you woke up today
But you couldn't stop flirtin'
Any fears you downplayed

I looked in your eyes
So trusting they are
As I said my goodbye
I knew you weren't going far

You walked to your room
In the giant hospital
Never looked back with gloom
Not even a little

I promise you'll feel better
When you wake up at noon
We'll sit down together
And bay at the moon

I said, don't be afraid
As you closed your sweet eyes
I'll soon cross the bridge
To see my sweet Maximus

© *Stefanie Fletcher, April 2020*

PROMPT #12

Literally overnight our world turned upside down. Everything that defined us as people is no longer safe. PDA is a definite no-no. Think about what life was like before this lockdown and what it is like now. How does it feel to be denied any human connection? What do you miss the most about your life BC, before COVID-19?

When you are ready, write poetically about how life has changed since the lockdown.

POEMS INSPIRED BY PROMPT #12

No More Time for BS

I stopped thinking that life was forever after cancer,
I changed,
I learned how to seize the moment,
But I still put other people's feelings before my own,
I deferred when I really wanted to run,
I allowed little things to bother me,
I put other people before me,
COVID-19 has changed all that,
Thank God,
Life really is too short to sweat the small things,
Isolation has made me prickly,
I used to keep my mouth shut,
No more,
Now I talk,
And sometimes people don't like what I have to say,
Other times I don't like what they have to say,
Now I don't defer,
I don't run away,
I don't even have to walk,
All I do is defriend,
And if that doesn't work,
There is always the atomic weapon,
Blocking people,
My block list grows every day,
When there is no social contact,
We are left with social media,
Where would we be now without Zoom or Facebook,
Zoom has grown from 20 million users in December 2019 to 200 million users,
If that is not proof that we are social creatures,
What is?
I miss touching other people,
Not in a sexual way,
Just simple human contact,
I miss playing with other people's dogs,
I miss hugs,
Today I was told that I had COVID-19 and I am recovered,
I feel incredibly blessed,
I was lucky,
Lots of other people have not been so lucky,
I pray that we can all bump into each other without fear of contamination,
I look forward to not crossing the street,
Until then,
Thank God for Zoom.

© Howard Kern, March 2020

Luxury Touch

I was wrapped in a warm embrace of the most delicious kind,
Touch was my magic in every aspect,
I could and I can feel the tiniest tight muscle with my feet,
I'm confined to only two now,
I LOVE TOUCHING MY FACE,
And the faces of other people,
Tracing the lines of the brow,
And the third eye,
The temples,
And above and below the lips,
I really miss it,
I miss the possibility,
The mystery of anything can happen.
Of the unknown being more than trying to manage a fear,
It was an adventure.

© *Phoebe Diftler, April 2020*

PROMPT #13

Three weeks done and maybe one more month to go. There is an expression that "man plans and God laughs." But there is another expression, "nothing ventured, nothing gained." Think about what you would like to achieve on any level, personal, business, whatever, during the next four weeks. Be aspirational and do not allow your mind to limit your imagination. On paper, anything is possible.

When you are ready, write about how you can make these next four weeks valuable for the rest of your life.

POEMS INSPIRED BY PROMPT #13

My Life in Pictures

I thought—What can I organize that I never have time to?
So I chose one thing
My print photograph collection
The 5 massive bins of prints sitting in my attic
That document my life and my mother's life
My father's life and the first seven years of my oldest son's life
And the first year of my younger son's life
Our life before marriage and our life before children
Our travels and our milestones

It seemed so appropriate to do this now
While I have all of this time
It's meaningful and meditative
Viewing the images of togetherness
Brings joy and sadness
Times of closeness—No distance
Appreciating and savoring them all
Paris, Belgium, Venice, London, Munich, Rome and Tokyo
Will my children ever go?

Realizing how blessed I have been to see all of these places
Wondering when and how can I ever wish to go
On a plane again

Grateful for my obsession with photography
And for these documents of my life
Treasuring all of them though a daunting task

These thousands of photographs
Holding them in my hands
The doubles and the negatives
The slides, the color, the faded and the black and white

All telling stories
Snapshots of times that were
Wondering about times to be
Grieving those that have passed away
And realizing I cannot do this every day

© Jenifer Winters, O'Neill April 2020

Always A Butterfly

I asked my grandchildren to make me lots of butterflies to decorate my house,
I've longed for a retreat for many years,
To go always to a quiet spot and reflect,
Presto! COVID-19,
You've given me my wish!
How could I be so incredibly lucky?!
So . . . what to do at this retreat?

Playing.
I was going to say,
"Practicing piano.
Learning to play and improving."
But the truth is I'm messing about and just simply playing,
Like when you're a kid playing.
Early on I felt guilty and made a list of chores I could check off . . .
Those sorts of things I never seem to get around to,
Cleaning under the bed,
Clearing a closet,
Fixing a few items,
Organizing the remainder of the garage,
Hmm . . .
I honestly believe it doesn't matter how long COVID lasts,
Those things will still be there,
Waiting to be done when It's over.

I've been working on sleeping,
Relaxing,
Enjoying the sheer luxury of feeling how incredibly cozy my pillows are,
Waking up early, as always, and thinking,
"Who cares? I have no place to be, I might as well sleep in,"
I haven't afforded myself this opportunity in a long time.

I'm getting stronger,
I had already purchased a Peloton bike (with lots of classes) just prior to being
    quarantined,
I love beating my own personal records,
It's fun!

POEMS INSPIRED BY PROMPT #13

(continued)

I love having nothing to show for myself,
Too many years spent overachieving,
Today I watched a hummingbird,
And I've been stalking a returning Western Jay,
Sometimes I don't answer my FaceTime,
And fake like my phone ran out of charge,
Or that I left it downstairs,
I let people worry this lapse is due to age related mental deterioration.

In my fantasy,
I emerge from this month or two as totally fit,
Like one of those before & after shots,
I'll have miraculously jumped from being a late beginner/early intermediate piano player,
To being able to play beside concert pianists,
But, then I think,
". . . you'll be pretty close to the same, maybe a tiny bit better on both the fitness and piano front,"
It's all good,
In between,
I've watched a bit of delightfully trashy television.

I have no desire—well,
In honesty,
I still have twinges of
"And what, EXACTLY, do you have to show for yourself, Young Lady?"
And my reply,
"Nothing at all!
Nope, not one thing!"
BUT, as you might notice,
I still came out a butterfly,
All I had to do was let Nature take her course.

© *Deborah Williams, April 2020*

Life Is But A Dream

Someone once tasked me:
"Describe yourself in a single word."

"JOY," I said,
(immediately)

Because

Beneath, beside,
Above, below—
Joy is every direction
And I want you to feel it.

Joy is choice.
Vision is choice.

Yes, yes, my rose-colored glasses—
(Before, after, and yes NOW)

Because really, Anyway, there is and was
And only ever will be now.

You're alive now.
You're safe now.
Be happy now.

© *Ruth Waytz, March 2020*

PROMPT #14

We are sociable people. We live in community. However, we are being directed by our government leaders to avoid unnecessary contact with other people. This directive goes against the human condition. Some of us may be enjoying the seclusion. However, others may be climbing up a wall. Which category are you in? Do you know anyone who is climbing up a wall? Think about what you would like to say to yourself or that other person to calm the nerves and let whomever know that everything will be alright.

When you are ready begin to write poetically and from the heart kind words to calm the fears of any person that is out there that may be struggling with this forced isolation.

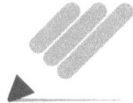

POEMS INSPIRED BY PROMPT #14

Vacant Schedule Filled

I awake,
I think,
No, I don't want to think,
Unwelcomed thoughts,
Unearthed thoughts,
Unresolved thoughts,
Awake,
This COVID silence,
Louder.
Pounding and pounding in the corridors of my soul,
Silence turns up the noise,
Within,
Silence turns up the unresolved,
Within,
Stop!
Leave my brain,
Think,
Think about what?
You know what,
No.
Not now,
Then when?
I don't know.
Not, now,
Now!
Leave!
This quiet,
Never ending silence,
Forces me to think,
Forces me to see,
My vacant schedule,
Filled with ancient moments,
Unresolved moments,
Aching to be unearthed,
Back to earth,
Back up for air,
Back up to make noise,
Unresolved moments,
Haunt me,
My dreams,
My daydreams,
Haunt me in the silence of waiting.

© Christina Helena, April 2020

You've Been Through Worse

It is easy to be down and dreary,
Being positive all the time can grow weary,
But in times of woe,
Don't let go of times not so long ago,
Cancer was the word of the day,
But somehow you found your way,
Then there was economic malaise,
Or so they say,
You never said die,
You did not even wonder why,
Tears shed for so much loss,
But agony is not the boss,
Joy will find its way,
And the dogs will one day play,
Today there are clouds in the sky,
But even viruses have to die,
You have the cure for so much sadness,
We do not have to subscribe to all this madness,
Part your lips to beguile,
And share your hope and love with your beautiful smile.

© Howard Kern, April 2020

PROMPT #15

With modern technology we can always be connected. However, sometimes we are alone. Who or what fills your time when you are not having a Zoom cocktail or are on the phone with someone? Think about how that person or thing has been your salvation as many of us celebrate either the Easter or Passover holidays.

When you are ready, begin to write poetically of your gratitude for your Savior, whoever or whatever that is.

POEMS INSPIRED BY PROMPT #15

Bow Wow and Meow

I am never alone,
Every moment of the day I am surrounded by sounds,
Meow,
Meow,
Meow,
Time to eat,
Woof woof,
There's someone walking by,
Scratch scratch,
I want some fresh air,
"Only kidding,
I wanted you to get out of your chair,
This constant lying around is boring me to death so me thinks,"
Or so I think she thinks,
Meow,
Meow,
Woof woof,
Meow,
Meow,
A constant cacophony of love,
Abbreviated by the welcome sleep at the end of each locked-in day,
I am not alone,
My animal companions constantly remind me of that,
When I sit at my desk,
My 85 pound dog rebels,
She grabs my arms to pull me away from work mode,
Until she finally finds her spot on my lap,
Alone,
Not me,
My pets constantly remind me that I am loved,
And though the lock-down has disrupted many lives,
My pets don't seem to mind,
Woof woof woof,
Meow meow meow,
Scratch scratch scratch,
My life in lock-down,
No wonder people are adopting animals at a record pace right now,
Beautiful sounds of domesticated nature,
A constant reminder that I am loved,
Got to go,
Nature calls.

© Howard Kern, April 2020

For the Love of Dog

I am blessed with many saviors during this lockdown
Plentiful food, access to fresh air and nature
But the biggest savior
Is my little dog

Her fuzzy unconditional love and longing gazes
Always ready for a belly rub
These all take me away
From thoughts of doom
Worry and sadness
She knows none of this

Her silent gratitude for feedings and snacks
The baths and brushing
And even her two-legged housemates
Is a healing force

Taking long walks with her
Has freed me
Helped me stay active
And taken me into nature
And she's always ready
Her ears perk up at the words "go" and "walk"

Just her presence is calming, reassuring to me and my family
The joy she brings is saving us all
Every day.

© *Jenifer Winters O'Neill, April 2020*

PROMPT #16

Some say that you can never say "I love you" enough. Reasonable folks can disagree. However two words that bring a smile to my face are "thank you." We all have many people to thank during this epic time. Think about who you would like to thank.

When you are ready, poetically write a warm thank you to whomever your heart directs.

POEMS INSPIRED BY PROMPT #16

The Concrete Canyons

The concrete canyons
Echo with the sound of one hand clapping.

The constant din.
The bustling traffic.
Now nothing more than a muscle memory.
You could pee in the middle of Broadway
And not risk getting run over.

Out for some air.
Six feet apart.
Nice hair.
Great ass.
Wonder what she looks like under that mask.

The punk on the skateboard comes whizzing by.
No mask.
No gloves.
His only protection, ear buds.
Oblivious to the reality around him.
I want to punch the little motherfucker in the gut.
Is his grandmother in her apartment alone?
His grandfather in a nursing home?
Maybe dying?
Some surely are.

Then, seven o'clock rolls around.
Windows open
And suddenly the canyons are filled with sound.

Reverberating now
Hundreds of hands clapping.
People cheering.
Music blaring.
Pots and pans clanging.
All in cacophonous tribute
To the heroes on the front line
Risking it all
While we stay safe inside.

Ten minutes and it's over.
But we'll do it again,
Tomorrow.

© *Jeffrey Altshuler, April 2020*

Dementia, Dad, and COVID-19

This ShiftPoem is dedicated to my mom, whose body is failing her rapidly, while her mind remains sharp.

I can't thank him,
How can I even talk about him now?

My hero,
My Oak Tree,
My Dad.

He lived in our family home for a lifetime,
His mind finally too old to care for it,
His memory fading like an ebbing tide,
Forced to cede his chain saw and tractor to age and illness,
His boat and trailers, rifle, rod, and icehouse—
He can't keep "them keys" straight
30 of them laid out on the trunk of his 1960 Thunderbird.
What key starts which motor goes to what lock?
His three sons inventing thirteen different methods
Of mnemonic prompting to no avail—
He looks confused moving in his bathrobe slowly
From his chair where he fell asleep reading the paper
For sixty years every day after work to a luxury condo at Epiphany Church.

These were going to be his "golden years,"
More like his final act.
I stay with him and mom for two months every summer
Cooking, cleaning up, managing the meds, the bills
Giving my siblings a bit of a break.
I wanted to see him this summer too,
I wanted to stay on the ship until the final whistle,
But my visit was interrupted by a strangely quiet storm:
A pandemic,
Something that passes through this world once in a century,
COVID-19 has kept my dad from me,
These precious moments stolen by strong suggestion of the State:
Shelter in Place in my apartment far away from the man who raised me.

I can't think about him locked in a luxury condo with mom,
Unable to leave their room, say, to walk the halls,
Quarantined in this strange and viral time,
Ironically imprisoned in the church he dug the foundation for in 1964.

POEMS INSPIRED BY PROMPT #16

(continued)

His mind is going,
His autonomy tumbling into monotony and befuddlement
They took the keys to his truck,
After he wrecked the second one, he's forsaken
The many small engines he tuned and oiled.
Quiet now are his snow-plow and ice-augur.
For the scythe of age is come, inevitable, like cold
In a Minnesota winter. He makes shit up.
Vandals removing the stairs from his house
So he can't get a sleeping bag from the basement.
Kidnappers stealing his wallet and hiding it inside the ceiling light fixture.
His mind riding the anxiety train in nightmarish jumbles
And it's all as real as breathing. He can't tell the difference.

COVID-19
Dementia
Lockdown

His belongings stuffed in paper bags he stands ready
At the door of the condo
For when this thing ends
He wants to go home

But they found him without his phone and his wallet
Standing in the park about a half mile from the condo
A week before the quarantine.
He didn't know his name and he wasn't sure where he was going.
If my older brother hadn't found him . . .

But all he wants to do is water the trees
he planted as saplings.
Now these giants are mighty Ash, Spruce and Maple
With trunks that need the arms of three men to encircle.

But there are two he didn't plant—
he once saved two great big Red Oaks
From certain death as a lethal fungus
Devastated dozens in our front yard forest when I was a boy
It was a pandemic for trees called Oak Wilt.

He drove a long pointed metal rod
(I remember I was nine)
Twenty feet down into the roots

(continued)

In a giant circle and pouring
A chemical he sent away for down the holes
He protected those two trees from the fungus.
Something like two hundred and fifty holes
Took us two days.
You should see them now, more than
A century old and towering over the house
He's now compelled to vacate and sell.

Life used to be so simple,
Cutting the afternoon grass surrounding his home,
After catching a fish dinner from the lake at dawn.
He tended all (including us) for half a century.
You should see his shoe shine kit.

He was my light,
My knight in shining armor,
He taught me what dads teach their sons,
I could not have asked for a better teacher.

But now our conversations twist and dwindle
Even with my finishing his sentences he loses his thread
Makes shit up or worse,
He is silenced
by COVID-19 and dementia,

I don't bring up fishing,
Ice or otherwise,
He nods off fifty-odd times a day,
When you can see him
tying fishing hooks in his sleep,
His ancient fingers moving in remembered loops and tugs,

It hurts me to watch this sad dream-dance,
But what good is it to look away?

The last time we fished Sturgeon Lake
North of Ignace, Canada,
He kept dropping his rod in the back of the boat
I'd turn from the bow and see him sleeping
A walleye tap tapping his line bouncing the end of his rod
Threatening to pull his whole rig into the lake. Wake up, Dad, Set the Hook.

POEMS INSPIRED BY PROMPT #16

(continued)

Late that same afternoon, pulling into the dock
he looks up at me and says
"Who are you?"

"I'm Mark dad, you know me,
Markle Sparkle, your second son
The one that moved away to New York."
After a confused silence he says with assurance:
"You look like Mark."

Later, cleaning fish at the counter he pretends it was a joke to save face.
"Had ya goin' there din't I?"
"Yeah, Dad, you sure did, you had me going."

No longer in the house he built back in 1968,
Alone with my mom in a luxury condo,
A mind inventing disasters and darkness
thanks to COVID-19 and dementia,
Nature,
In all its beauty,
Can be cruel.

Left with memories of time gone by,
I'm not able to share his breath for fear of killing him,
When will all this end?
Will I be able to hold his hand before he breathes his last breath?
Will we ever fish together again?
My hero,
My Oak Tree,
My Dad.

Last summer I remember fixing an outlet in his basement,
He didn't know which end of the wrench was open,
No longer the master mechanic,
He was Mr. Fix anything,
He could weld anything,
He was MacGyver without the explosions,
All he needed was a swiss army knife and a paperclip,
Gravity and a lever.

(continued)

He was Mr. Make-Do,
He could grease anything,
Start anything,
Catch anything,
A life spent making the wheel go round.

Funny what you remember when all you have are memories,
Living in a luxury condo with mom,
Separated by COVID-19 and dementia.

I would get in trouble when I was a little kid and held the light in his eyes,
Now it doesn't matter, though he's shining it in mine as we fix the outlet in the dark.
The light passes through,
No more awareness, then a glimmer
The light coming and going in his eyes,
In a rare moment of clarity he says,
"Son, soon I'm going to owe you my life,"
I choke back a sob,
"What are you talking about?" I say, barely able to speak,
"Who do you think taught me to do all this?"

My hero,
My Oak Tree,
My Dad.
Living in a luxury condo with mom,
Separated by COVID-19 and dementia.

© Mark Schulte, April 2020

PROMPT #17

As we get older, death and dying become a more common occurrence in our lives. It is unusual that the whole world is sharing this sensation at the same time, but here we are. We either know someone who is sick or have read about strangers who are sick. This is a tragedy because we want the whole world to be healthy. But that is not real. Every single person alive at this moment is going to die. We all are going to die. The question is how are we going to live? What do you still want to do in your life? What would you regret the most if you passed away tomorrow?

When you are ready, write poetically and from the heart about the things you still want to achieve in this lifetime.

POEMS INSPIRED BY PROMPT #17

Vast Ellipses of Time

What happens in the interstices?
Shadow boxing with the future.
Waiting is.
Waiting is.

Are we even halfway through? And
What do I content myself with? Where
Do I insert the pieces from this
Bottomless bag of commas?
Do I eat better, watch TV, keep a journal, read a book,
And fret, and fret, and fret
In between vast ellipses of time that
Stretch out endlessly.

What is the structure in between?
How can I construct
Meaning when all the punctuation is gone?
The vital dashes of
Strained commutes, the
Brief semicolon of a lunch spot in Midtown, the
Parentheses of rushed conversations at work, some
Tidbit of gossip, or a
Catch-up chat between classes.

My life is a run-on sentence, and
The clauses are bunching up,
Dependent, independent,
Complete thoughts and fragments
Scattered in between a
Vast field of ellipses like
Ripples across a still, deep sea.

I'm swimming in an ocean of time, and
What is my mind doing?
Racing to where?
What conclusions can I draw when
Time seems to have been suspended,
Bunched up,
Five minutes, five seconds,

Eternity in an hour,
Who knows when
Ellipses like pebbles scattered
Disturb a placid surface, glass, still but
Vibrating now with an anxious, failing breath . . .
What do we do in the spaces in between?
Read books, look for something to worry about, pick a fight, take a long hot shower and
Toss ideas like sticks clicking in our minds.

(continued)

Time is a sea scattered with rocks like
Ellipses, small footholds where
Perhaps
I can see, dotted there, some path.

© *Michelle Koza, April 2020*

More to Do

Ever since I can remember,
I've experienced the thousand faces of fear,
Fear of Nature—
Fear of Nighttime—
Fear of Flying—
Fear of Women—
Fear of Men—
Fear of People—
Fear of Success—
Fear of Failure and more . . .
I've made amazing inroads into these themes,
But there's more to do,
What I still want to do—
I want to know more Peace—
more Beauty—
more Goodness,
Do I need to travel to do that?
Maybe . . . my return to Vietnam,
Where I experienced the "limits of human experience"
Transforming my perceptions of those people,
There and myself,
And shed light on old fears,
When I was in Vietnam all I thought about was living,
After I got home,
All I thought about was dying,
What do I want to do now?
I want to absorb as much life as there is to live,
I want my senses to discover and apply as much as they can to my life,
And of course,
I want to learn to be as happy as possible beyond my fears—
or with them,
The Ancient Greeks say,
Definition of Happiness—Making full use of your powers along the lines of excellence.

© *Brian Delate, April 2020*

PROMPT #18

Some of us have dealt with illness and survived. Some of us live with illness. It is a very unusual experience when all of humanity is faced with its mortality at the same time. That is what we all are facing with the Coronavirus. However, even the most pessimistic doctor recognizes that the vast majority of us will get through this pandemic. Instead of being scared or pessimistic, recognize your power and write a letter to yourself as to why you will get through this pandemic. Positive thinking has never hurt anyone.

Love yourself and tell yourself that you are special and you will not only survive, but you will thrive as a valuable human being.

When you are ready, write this poem to the most special person in the Universe, you.

POEMS INSPIRED BY PROMPT #18

Thank You Deborah

Thank you, Deborah,
For giving me this crazy, fun, adventure filed life!
Thank you for all the little things you do to take care of the future me,
Those little presents—
I found two in the freezer today,
We're having them for dinner,
Gorgeous stuffed red peppers,
You made too many the first time,
Saying "the extras are a little gift for the future us."
You even said,
"I don't know when I'll eat these, but the future 'you' will say 'thank you for your thoughtfulness!'
It'll be a day when she doesn't cook but wants a wholesome, home cooked meal,"
That day has arrived and I say,
"Thank you!"

Thank you for noticing that, sometimes,
other care can overtake self-care,
Thank you for always being aware of when I'm out of balance,
And being willing to readjust - to say "no, thank you" to others,
To create the space for me.

Thank you for being the kid that did her own thing—
Regardless of whether it held promise for monetary success,
And, who knew?!
It all just followed,
And everything worked out perfectly!
Better than you could've ever dreamed!

Thank you for being optimistic and taking chances,
Thank you for always keeping the end in mind - for saying,
"This life is limited. This will pass. What is of most importance?"
Thank you for being present—
embedding all those wonderful "nows" into so many vivid memories,
Thank you for noticing all the wonder and beauty right here,
It will remain.

© *Deborah Williams, April 2020*

Thank You

I don't know who I will be talking to,
Hopefully God,
But I know the only thing left to say at the end will be thank you,
Thank you for giving me my family and my friends
Thank you for giving me my mind and my body and most importantly,
Thank you for giving me my heart
You blessed me with compassion,
I am so lucky that I care about people,
I crave community,
I want to see people,
All kinds of people.
My life is enriched by shared experiences,
I have no desire to conquer or defeat others,
But,
I get jealous
I covet what others have
I see that guy on TV playing the part I should have gotten
The girl on the vacation I should have been on.
The person with their boyfriend who should be with me
I get mean,
With telephone reps who won't give me what I want
With the parking attendant who won't let me idle for five minutes while I run in to grab my to go order
With myself when I don't behave in the way I should
Or I don't succeed at the task in front of me.
But, in the grand scheme of things
Those are the distractions not the truth of who I am at my core.
I am the boy who sat with his friend on the phone for three hours and helped him work through an emotional breakdown, instead of finishing his math homework
I am the man who worked with his roommate and his roommate's girlfriend until they saw the true beauty of what they have together.
And there is more to my truth,
God, you gave me the ability to listen to others, and give them a safe space to explore,
The vulnerability to love with my whole heart and the desire of wanting to be loved back
You gave me, the trust that humanity will take care of me and the tools to return the favor
And while you have given me the opportunity to celebrate their wins
The real reason you brought me here is to celebrate in their growth,
Their triumph over their demons.

POEMS INSPIRED BY PROMPT #18

(continued)

And the realization that they can accomplish things they never thought were possible.
You have made me a vessel of the reality of infinite possibilities
Enough food on the table for all.
Enough space for everyone to feel happy and loved
And you left space in my heart for the darker part of humanity,
Both in myself and others

You have shown me my share of darkness and demons,
Evil,
Suffering and sadness,
But you have carried me through those hard times,
And the messages, in those moments, were always the same,
Cry harder,
Feel harder,
Love harder,
And you will get through this,
Here I sit locked up in my apartment,
Deprived of human companionship except what I share on Zoom,
But you give me hope
That even in these uncertain times
You will allow me to continue to be your peaceful warrior of truth and love,
A love machine always raring to get started,
And what better way to say thank you to my creator than to be real,
To be true,
And to live this life that you gifted me to the fullest,
So one more time,
But not for the last time,
Thank You,
Thank You,
Thank You.

© *Jesse Pudles, April 2020*

Smacked Up: Inadequate

Awe and inspiration come,
As they are triumphant,
In their ordinary clothes.
They don't give up,
Despite oceans of power
Over them mountains of pain,
They persevere.

Predictable Underdog complex:
When Polly's in trouble I am not slow,
It's hip hip Up and away I go.
But in the secret compartment of my ring I fear
my brokenness will keep me here
like a pimp his hooker
Smacked up on something.

But this is what awes me:
My own fear of what
I wish I knew.

Not giving up I am
stubbornness.

Nature lately is my sole comfort,
Beauty left the museum alone
A long time ago and found me
by the sea moving rocks
Or words on the train like rhymes
In a drop down goddess menu.

© Mark Schulte, April 2020

PROMPT #19

It has been a month since we have been under siege by COVID-19. You made it this far and hopefully the end is in sight. Think about this past month and the unexpected gifts you may have received.

When you are ready, begin to write poetically about the positive things you experienced over the past month.

POEMS INSPIRED BY PROMPT #19

Reconnecting

Out of the ethers,
Born of isolation,
Some old friends came.
Nearly forgotten names
On the heading
Of an email chain.

Faded memories,
Sketched by the pen of the soul,
Long passed,
Who linked us all.
Happily shared by those who knew him.

Caricatures on horseback
Trotting across the screen
In poses askew and extreme.
Impressions of moments long gone.
But each with its own background song.

Reminders of a cherished past.
Played out to the rhythm of a horse's hoofbeats.
Nice to remember
Nice to be remembered

In these flashbacks the spirit lives on.
Old victories.
Old horses.
Old friends.
Old lovers.

We're all older now
But the trick of these times . . .

Stay old
Not dead

© *Jeffrey Altshuler, April 2020*

Newfound Old Friends

I have more good friends than I thought,
So many people have reached out
—called—
Zoomed—
FaceTimed,
It's so nice these virtual meetings!

I've learned "The Entertainer" on the piano,
It's slow - but I'm building speed,
I just started another song - "Stormy Weather"
I really love these old songs,
I've virtually taught my grandchildren the song (including all the verses) to
   "How Much is That Doggie in the Window?"

I've enjoyed cooking,
Normally, I'm very perfectionistic about preparation and ingredients,
I've returned to my roots and am just making do with whatever is on hand,
It's nice.

I've fallen more and more in love with my dog!
How funny is he when all he does all day is lay beside me sleeping,
Just when he sees we're headed to bed in the evening,
He sprints as quickly as possible to his bed,
Which is right next to ours!

I've seen my husband at work—something I've never really been privy to,
He works very hard and all day,
I walk in quietly and bring him tea,
Only hearing snippets,
It's still clear how great he gets along with everyone and how much he wants to
   help everyone succeed.

POEMS INSPIRED BY PROMPT #19

(continued)

I'm enjoying my house,
I found things in my garage I didn't know were there,
I've just relaxed and am not worrying about getting anything accomplished,
I've watched a bit of television (actually, not as much as I would like!),
I've seen shows I would normally never see
—like, "Tiger King"—
What a bizarre story—recommended by others with lots of time on their hands!

Mostly, I've just truly enjoyed being well & healthy.

© Deborah Williams, April 2020

Wonder in Mysterious Ways

You work in such mysterious ways,
You have a plan,
Things are meant to be,
You show me signs along the way,
Coincidences that simply cannot be,
You give me hope,
You are everything and more,
I give thanks to the Universe.

© Jeffrey Hollander, April 2020

PROMPT #20

We are living in extraordinary times. Some of our loved ones did not make it to 2020. What would you like to tell them about life in lock-down? What would you like them to tell you to provide comfort that you have been missing? Whether it is death or quarantine, we all find ourselves separated from loved ones.

When you are ready, write poetically to your departed loved ones about the good and the bad of being in isolation.

POEMS INSPIRED BY PROMPT #20

Letter to Karen

Dear Karen,

Well, you're not missing anything with this virus,
If you are watching,
I'll bet you're amused,
And if you're watching our daughter,
Which I feel you are,
Then you must be so proud of her journey with completing her MFA next month,
But, oh, my,
How she still misses you!

Missing You,
Brian

. . .

Dear Brian,

I miss you and Tirsa all the time,
It's been four years since I had to leave,
Time is very different here,
My heart is thrilled to see you give her the reassurance she sometimes needs,
Both worlds—this one and that one are filled with love,
It's more of a challenge there,
But it can be such a beautiful staging arena for what's to follow,
Believe me,
You're a survivor and so is our daughter,
Don't stop experiencing the Joy!
That's what it's all about.

Your Guardian Angel,
Karen

© *Brian Delate, April 2020*

Whaddaya Say, Whaddaya Say, Whaddaya Say

Hey Kerry,
So how is it up there in heaven?
Maybe I'm being presumptuous,
But my bet is you made the cut,
Your birthday just passed,
You would have been 63,
Same age as my older brother,
I can't believe it's been over six years,
Time sure flies when you're alive,
Just kidding,
I shouldn't joke with you,
You may haunt me,
I remember some of your practical jokes,
They were harsh when you were alive,
I can't imagine what they would be like with unearthly powers,
I'm not afraid,
You were always my friend,
You would not believe what's been going on since you've been gone,
Do you remember Donald Trump?
He's now President Donald Trump,
Really,
It's like watching sur-reality TV,
Don't worry,
He won't be joining you,
The Beatles sang about a Ticket to Ride,
Trump has a Ticket to Hell,
And poor Kobe Bryant,
He was controversial as a basketball player,
But he was great in retirement,
He even won an Oscar,
Unfortunately he and his daughter and seven other people died in a helicopter crash,
They probably made it up to see you,
But the most bizarre thing is this COVID-19,
A killer without a conscience,
I thought of you because of the respirators,
They are life-savers,
Or in most cases,
End-of-life savers,

POEMS INSPIRED BY PROMPT #20

(continued)

It's sad,
I wish you were here to talk to,
You always knew what to say,
Even when the ALS crippled your body,
And you spoke in a woman's voice through the synthesizer,
You could make me feel better,
I miss you buddy,
I don't know that I'll make it up to your parts,
But one can dream,
Stay inside and stay well,
Maybe not applicable to you,
I miss you my friend.

© *Howard Kern, April 2020*

A Letter to Murray on his 78th Birthday

You didn't make it to 2020
You barely made it to 2019
You were ravaged
Taken quickly by cancer
A disease our society knows all too well
Cruel to people of all ages—
Maybe you had the underlying health issues
For a long, long, time!
But once you "felt it"
You went poof.
And chose to let go.

Tributes to you flooded in
And I write this poem on what would have been
Your 78th birthday

Big brother
You would not have wanted to be around
For what is happening now
Greed, political distraction
A lack of consideration for human life
For the life of the planet
It's all dovetailing to gift us—
With a virus—A disease—
Cropping up all over the world

(continued)

Folks are self-isolating all around the globe
Wearing facemasks and other protective gear
We are washing our hands madly, never touching our faces
Now we have a new societal mode called "social distancing"
Stay at least 6 feet away from everyone all the time
Maybe forever?

What doesn't kill you makes you stronger—
The world is so connected these days—
Business is global
But the international travel it inspires—
Gives the virus wings to fly

Hopefully we will
Rid ourselves of this pandemic
Called COVID-19
It's after us over Sixties—
Especially those with underlying health issues
Who doesn't have underlying health issues??!!

You would have been a moving target for this killer
Like the rest of us, your closest running mates

I tested positive
I had the virus but in a very mild form
I was spared the fever, chills, and lethal respiratory inhibition
Instead I have a lack of energy (no kidding)
And fuzzy brain (not habit forming)
I lost my sense of taste—a drag—
Alternately I eat everything in sight
In search of texture and viscosity
Or eat nothing— cause it sure ain't worth the effort

Yes, I deflect with my usual oddball sense of humor
You did always call me your own Ellen DeGeneres

I miss you too much, dear Murray

And one final note from Paul Simon:

"A broken laugh a broken fever
Take it up with the great deceiver
Who looks you in the eye
And says baby don't cry
Further to fly"

© *Barbara Ligeti, April 2020*

PROMPT #21

All of us can have great thoughts that never get heard. But sometimes, just putting a thought out in the Universe can lead to great change. Think about this pandemic and what you would do differently. Maybe your thoughts would lead to positive change. All of us are important and we all can make a difference.

When you are ready, write poetically about how you would improve the world in the time of COVID-19.

POEMS INSPIRED BY PROMPT #21

If I Were King

If I had all the power in the world,
I would surround myself with people from all walks of life,
Paupers to princes,
Scientists to janitors,
Mannered gentry to the homeless,
I would want to hear from everyone so that the opinions would not be skewed by wealth or privilege,
People would be able to pee in whatever bathroom they felt comfortable in,
Sit or stand,
It would make no difference,
I would provide housing for the homeless,
Everyone would be able to serve their respective purposes,
People would be judged on merit and not on bank balances,
Discrimination would be addressed with compassion and not with more hatred,
And if my empire was ever faced with a pandemic,
I would gather the greatest minds from around the world to battle the pandemic,
I would give the podium to these doctors and scientists and ask them to lead our people to safety,
I would admit my mistakes and correct them,
I would not deny them to save my precious ego,
Ralph Kramden once said to Alice,
"I am King and you are nothing,"
Alice responded,
"Great Ralph, you are King over nothing,"
If I let my people die,
I will be left with nothing,
Happiness like all good things in life needs to be shared,
Finally,
I would relinquish my throne and let the people pick a leader amongst themselves,
And I would live happily knowing the Universal truth,
God,
Yahweh,
Allah,
Jesus,
Buddha,
The Universe,
I was never really king,
No person is,
Because there always is a greater power than ourselves,
Ashes to ashes,
Dust to dust,
We start out the same,
We end the same,

(continued)

But somehow the world keeps on going,
Sorry Donny,
No human is king,
Even if millions of people believe otherwise,
Mother Nature always wins.

© *Howard Kern, April 2020*

We Shall Overcome

Martin Luther King said it best,
"We shall overcome,"
Countless choirs across America have put it to Gospel music,
So simple yet seemingly so far away,
It's hard to accept that when we read about more and more people dying every day,
It's hard to accept that when our leader misleads us for months instead of
consulting doctors and lessening the blow of this invisible invader,
We shall overcome,
Martin Luther King did not make it to 40,
Yet his teachings live on,
We shall overcome,
Some of us will perish,
Unnecessary death and suffering is heart wrenching,
We shall overcome,
We have great leaders that are paying attention,
Governors Cuomo, Newsom, and Whitmer to name a few,
We shall overcome,
Our doctors are paying attention,
They will not allow us to be put in harm's way even though the Orange ogre is
more concerned with his precious economy,
There is no joy where so many suffer needlessly,
What can you say to the hundreds of thousands that have buried loved ones,
It is not just the fatalities that die,
It is also the families and friends that are left behind,
Gold does not make everything right,
COVID-19 has changed a generation,
Children now have Pandemic days on top of snow days and sick days,
We are in the eye of the hurricane,
But as a great person once yelled,
We shall overcome.

© *Howard Kern, April 2020*

PROMPT #22

Imagine a world where sickness does not exist. Where your cupboards are full and you don't have to worry about whether there is enough TP.

That world existed before and it will exist again. But you don't have to wait for Uncle Sam to open the floodgates. You can recreate that world and maybe even make it better.

When you are ready, write poetically about what the world needs now . . .

POEMS INSPIRED BY PROMPT #22

Flowers

I will create with flowers and never stop.

To communicate only in the language of flowers,
Of color & scent, of oozing nectar & drifting pollen.

I will open my mouth and instead of words,
Flowers will come out as poetry, as music, as song.

I will decorate the earth with flowers and never stop,
Until I've made love in a flower, on top of a bed of flowers and underneath a canopy of flowers.

I will study the psychedelic, kaleidoscopic palette of flowers,
Until I know it from the perspective of a hummingbird or a honeybee,
So I can spread ultraviolet, aquamarine, infrared bliss across this world.

I will create with flowers and never stop.

My fingers will become paintbrushes and will paint flowers like vaginas to rival Georgia O'Keeffe.

My toes will become tap-shoes and will dance flowers, falling like a gentle Spring rain, to rival Gene Kelly.

"The Earth laughs in flowers," as Emmerson wrote,
And will I laugh in flowers too, so
Everyone will know the joy of creation alive in my heart,
gestating in my womb.

And when I've grown tired from creating with flowers, I'll nourish myself with flowers so I can start the cycle all over again.

Brunching on begonias at 11am,
Snacking on silversword at 2pm,
Dining on daffodils at 8pm.

I will stuff my face with flowers until my breath smells of jasmine and my poop literally smells like roses.

©*Jana Carrey, March 2020*

And You Will Never Tell Me Where to Pee

To all the People telling me to die;
For simply daring to live open. honestly. visibly.
You will never tell me where to pee.

Why must you feel so threatened?
Over something that will never affect you . . .
To all the People telling me to die;

You can sit down, be quiet
Because as long as I have my way . . .
You will never tell me where to pee.

Pass all the bills you like. Call me whatever name you can.
For I am unbreakable. Unable to be kept down.
To all the People telling me to die;

I am loud. I am proud. A champion for the voiceless and faceless
Small messages from behind a screen expressing words of thanks
You will never tell me where to pee.

So make me your martyr. Pour your hate on me like gasoline.
For when I am set ablaze, I will be reborn in the ashes again and again
To all the people telling me to die;
You will never tell me where to pee.

© *Peyton Ashby, April 2020*

PROMPT #23

Many people around the world are celebrating either freedom from slavery or the resurrection of their messiah. COVID-19 has locked all of us in either our homes or in fear. But as Martin Luther King said so eloquently, "We shall overcome." As humans, we are unique in the sense that we can show gratitude and we can celebrate the lives of others. Other species live one day at a time, and when a member of their tribe gets old or burdensome, he or she is left behind. We do not do that. In a perfect world, we would care for the infirm and celebrate the elderly. How lucky are we to be human? How fortunate are we to be able to show gratitude?

Think about the people that came before us that were enslaved. Who lived in squalor and in some cases sacrificed their lives so that we may be here today. We all can have a greater empathy for our ancestors and the hardships they endured. We may have different bodies but we are all the same.

When you are ready, write poetically to anyone who endured hardship and let that person know, "I get it now." What doesn't kill you makes you stronger. We all are going to be stronger and better people because we all will survive COVID-19.

POEMS INSPIRED BY PROMPT #23

Moses, Where Were You When We Needed You?

You led our people out of Egypt,
You were a great leader,
Or were you?
Story goes that your navigational skills were less than stellar,
First you lead everyone into the Red Sea,
Fortunately the Universe was kind,
And the Sea parted,
Lucky break or divine intervention?
Then you forgot to tell people to pack rations,
Again you lucked out,
Every morning the clothes are clean and manna appears from heaven,
And when people question your authority,
They get smitten,
Where's your sense of humor?
Finally it takes 40 years to find a parking spot,
Or should I say the "promised land?"
And none of your original followers survive the trip,
Not very impressive my friend,
You sound like our leader,
No sense of direction,
No tolerance for people that disagree,
And an inability to listen to opinions other than his own,
However times have changed,
We have governors like Whitmer and Cuomo and Newsom,
They are not afraid to lead and they listen to others,
I wonder what it would have been like if you would have listened to Aaron,
Or Miriam,
Or maybe even Kaleb,
The guy with the Golden Calf,
Too bad,
I guess we'll never know,
But I do know that I won't be wandering around for 40 years,
There is a Stay-at-home order,
Worst case scenario,
I'll just be stuck at home,
By the way,
This is what I learned from our fearful leader,
How to rewrite history,
Later,
Much.

© Howard Kern, April 2020

Grandma Berta

You came to America from the old country in 1929
With your four year old baby my daddy in tow
Also grandpa Jake whom you could never quite shake

The crash came in October and you said
"People still got to eat"
So you made delicious and cheap Eastern European food
Parlayed that into a delicatessen dynasty in two boroughs of New York

Your slender figure grew lumpy and lardy
From too much tasting I think
Your legs swelled from being on your feet night and day
Your face became ashen and lined due to worry and lack of sleep
You wore the same dress everyday – rinsing and wringing it out
 – a flag out to dry from your top floor tenement apartment
You always said "why have more than one dress when you can only wear one dress
    at a time"

You gave your son every advantage, lessons and schooling to
Become an engineer and designer and lover of music and art

While you toiled Jake drank and disappeared constantly
His greatest contribution to you, locking you out of the house
All night so you could learn to not forgetting your keys ever again

Dad traveled to Europe to stay with relatives while you set up stores in Cape
    Canaveral and Coco Beach Florida

He came back to the States and enlisted at the end of WWII for
Naturalized American citizenship

He was successful and passed privilege along to me –
But he drank to forget killing people as a sniper and he had
Flashbacks to how you and he were beaten
He couldn't help but squander some of life – but I never will –

Thank you Grandma B for love and for teaching me to
Make my own luck

© Barbara Ligeti, April 2020

PROMPT #24

COVID-19 and other times of stress can help us to see how ridiculous we or others can be. It is normal to see the irony of life even though we miss it when we are caught up in the daily treadmill. However, for many of us, the treadmill has stopped and we are left with videos of dogs playing, cats frolicking, and kids being.

When you are ready, begin to write poetically about things you have noticed that seem particularly amusing during this time of isolation.

POEMS INSPIRED BY PROMPT #24

I'm a Facebook Junkie

I am a Facebook Junkie
Good or bad—I am
I rely on it to stay connected
With friends and family
Favorite news outlets and brilliant writers
Historians and musicians

But true laughter has only come
When viewing the memes
Reading the sarcasm
Absorbing the wit
Relishing the humor
All to make light of our situation

I look forward to them each day
There have been dozens
All that poke fun
And make me think about
The time we have been given
The food I am eating
The ridiculousness of it all

I read them and share them
And feel great joy when I can
Bring a smile to someone's face
For it is laughter that helps me through

Sometimes I feel guilty
Having a laugh
When others are suffering so
But I savor the moments that I can let go

It heals my soul
And helps me forget what I don't know
For a moment

(continued)

I have a library of them now
The memes, the GIFs
The poems and funny photos
All reminders that laughter IS the best medicine

Whoever wrote that was right
In the bad we must see the light
And make light
To balance the darkness
And make delight
To balance the sadness

© *Jenifer Winters O'Neill April 2020*

POEMS INSPIRED BY PROMPT #24

Life Continues

I was driving the other day and saw a man getting a ticket on the highway,
I thought that was funny,
People are sick, scared, and dying,
And this poor sap gets a speeding ticket,
Life goes on,
Then I get home,
And there is a letter from the post office advising me that I am on notice,
The postman reported my dog as vicious,
Misidentifying her as a pitbull,
Claiming that she almost bit him,
I am outraged,
It doesn't matter that the world is upside down,
That our mindless leader talks and talks and talks and says nothing,
None of that matters,
The US Postal Service has declared war on my dog,
My beautiful mastiff mix breed accused of the impossible,
My yard is a fortress to protect the mailman,
The mailbox was moved away from the fence to create a safe social distance between him and the fangs of severe discomfort,
My dog is not perfect,
But who is?
My mind is now tuned in on animal injustice,
False accusations,
My dog has been #MeToo'd!
Where is the Crocodile Hunter when you need him?
Oh,
My bad,
He met his fate in the Great Barrier Reef,
I call the number on the letter,
Eerily marked Letter No. 1,
No answer,
The cowards must know I am calling,
Days pass,
My anger has not subsided,
There is no COVID-19,
Only this grave animal injustice,

(continued)

I finally see the mail truck,
It turns instead of coming to my house,
I fantasize that he is purposefully avoiding me,
I confront him,
He apologizes for the complaint,
He defended me to his superior even though he witnessed my dog's jaws of severe discomfort,
He is not my enemy,
He is my friend,
"What is your name?"
"Brandon,"
"How long have you had this route?"
"Five years,"
I put out my elbow for an introductory bump,
"I am Howard,"
I am ridiculous,
No more animal injustice,
Lucy is safe and secure,
Back to dealing with the real world,
Death and dying.

© Howard Kern, April 2020

PROMPT #25

Think about the world today, Coronavirus, masks, social-distancing, isolation, and think about how all these changes have affected not only you but the rest of society. Some of these changes may be temporary while others will be long-lasting.

When you are ready, write poetically about how you see all these changes going forward.

POEMS INSPIRED BY PROMPT #25

Amusing or Confusing

amusing or confusing
the handshake is obsolete
isn't that neat?
no more being judged
by your handle or your grip
it was a rip-off before
when you were expected to floor, or impress,
with a strong handshake
make a man in a c-suite
or a woman in a dress
quake as though
so much is at stake
through such a narrow
interaction, it's almost as if I'm watching
the last very last bastion
of the white patriarchy's hold
on form and fashion

amusing or confusing
the masks we wear
were they here
were they there
when we didn't put them on
but really come on
did we ever take them off
so much is at stake
through the fibers
and the fabric
if only this virus
would disappear like magic
as opposed to
the pandemonium
the pandemic leads us on
these harrowing moments tragic
we're practiced at being distant
socially until it's gone

amusing or confusing
shelter in place
don't get caught on the street
it's the ultimate disgrace
shamed for a walk
or a solitary stroll
to get a sip of java

(continued)

or to buy some berries for your bowl
whether just around the corner
or in the central mall plaza
so much is at stake
if you don't heed, obey
so amuse yourself somehow
stay at home is the way . . .

so much depends
on a red wheelbarrow
in the rain
amusing or confusing

only six feet away

© *Robert The Bench Galinsky, April 2020*

Castaway Time

I outlast solitude
through riff and rhyme

my fingers cocked
on pen ink shine

no cage no coop
no time to recoup

the clock I tossed
minutes are lost

the hour is what?
there came an early frost?

nothing is late
nor premature

in this quarantine
where time is cast away

of this one thing
I am sure

© *Robert The Bench Galinsky, April 2020*

POEMS INSPIRED BY PROMPT #25

Grateful

In the garden
my hands my nails
my knuckles my pails
are heavy with dirt
and the slivers don't hurt
       I'm Grateful

In bed I sleep I peep I creep
streaming serviced by
red wine done cheap
and red hairs on a bud
bold green and gleaming
soon eyelids closed
sealed for dreaming
       I'm Grateful

In the kitchen I cook
and I clean and I
finally fix the counter
it leaned to the left for years
and for no reason at all
I simply let it flounder
and now I'm home
I'm home I'm home
       I'm Grateful

In the shower I stand I bathe
sometimes with soap and suds
I pleasure and misbehave
with hot water and my privacy
I get myself in a lather
close my eyes
sing a song
and laugh at my own blather
       I'm Grateful

© *Robert The Bench Galinsky, April 2020*

Coping

Surrender is only to let Time's freshet flow past the iron grate
At its leisurely step, while the guardian pashas
drop edicts at our slovenly feet
And thrash the hesitant obeisance we offer.

Spiked iron manacles dig at every shuffle, and
We stare across the stripefilled yard, knowing our
Fellow travelers wander forever, while we just emerged
From a consumptive Black Maria into this Inferno.

Hoary grandfathers spake and we hid our faces:
This Alcatraz will take its chapter in the LIFE-compendium of
Holocausts, filled with panoplied supplicating multitudes of
Torched corpses, weeping siblings and gaunt hollow survivors.

Sitting at the emeraldclad table, do we play the red queen?
Beckoned, do we put on the deathmask and only whisper
Why? Let the rainbowed phoenix erupt from our
Breast and blast its bloody scream across the wasteland.

Yet does the indolent limpid stream meander past my muddy toes
While dear youths crowd this crammed corner and hide us from the
Blaring screen spouting babel, until we at last surfeit
And snuff out its raging flame.

Hector and Aeneas, Agamemnon and Achilles, Florence and Jeanne d'Arc,
gliding daily amongst the gaolyard, stalwart as the enormous oak trunk, patulent
As the ponderous branches, showering their loving embrace on
every miserable wretch. These valiants are the heroes for our time.

SURRENDER IS NO LONGER AN OPTION, WE SHALL PERSEVERE.

© Chas Timberlake, April 2020

PROMPT #26

Think about a struggle you faced before COVID-19 and how you resolved it. Now think about the struggles you may be facing in isolation, and how you can better yourself through these times when all we have are our thoughts.

When you are ready, write freely and allow your thoughts to guide you to a happier place.

POEMS INSPIRED BY PROMPT #26

Alone

I want to fall in love with being alone,
It's scary to admit because I love people,
But my heart of hearts knows my truth,
If I can fall in love with being alone,
There is no limit to what I can achieve.
Honoring alone,
Just me and my heart,
On a journey for the good,
But my resolve does not go untested,
I fear if I embrace alone,
I will be left that way,
I don't want to be left alone.
I want to fall in love with the silence in between the moments,
Where there is nothing to say and no one to talk to,
Can one truly experience love alone?
These are mere excuses,
My mind trying to prevent me from listening to my heart,
I want to fall in love with being alone so I can create space for others to fall in love with me,
Distance makes the heart grow fonder,
Or so they say,
There is something in this space that is so tangible yet ephemeral,
I want to be just as happy to have a full calendar as I am to find myself with an evening alone,
I want to fall in love with being single,
That's not an easy one to say,
Everything teaches us that we need a partner to feel complete,
Once I fall in love with alone,
That is when I will truly be ready for that partner,
That glorious moment when two people come together to create a single unit,
A new being,
Two people,
One soul,
Two hearts beating as one,
We all come into this world alone,
Once I can fall in love with the spaces in between,
Then I will truly be at peace,
I will truly get to appreciate being in a space together,
The truth is we are all connected, so we are never actually alone,
My fear of being alone isn't that at all
It's a fear of being lonely

(continued)

I don't want to be lonely,
The need to be with others creates a neediness that is not real,
Alone is perfection,
Coupling is perfection,
One is not better than the other,
But to form the perfect couple,
I need to allow space for each of us to be alone,
Alone together.
But not lonely,
That is love,
That is lovely,
That is perfection

© *Jesse Pudles, April 2020*

1918 vs. 2020

I think to 1918,
The flu that killed millions.
They too had to isolate.
A century later, we, their great great grandchildren,
face our own pandemic.

Back then, budding sweethearts couldn't FaceTime.
They lay in bed, imagining what their new love may be thinking.
The poker buddies had no online game.
The teenagers had no Zoom karaoke.
The masses had no Netflix in bed.
The lawyers couldn't Skype with clients.
Families had no Amazon to bring them face masks and hand soap,
no Instacart for groceries.

I look at my laptop and iPhone,
Cause of so much distraction and discord in our modern world.
And now they shimmer like gold.
Our source of entertainment, art and sustenance.
Our lifeblood to family and friends.
Our salvation, as we shelter and pray.

© *Kate Connor, April 2020*

PROMPT #27

One day COVID-19 will be in the past and we can all take a collective deep breath and celebrate life and actually start planning for our futures and finally exit "survival mode." While in isolation, we get to visit our thoughts and realize what we may have been missing in our lives.

When you are ready, write poetically and from the heart about what you are looking forward to Post-COVID-19.

POEMS INSPIRED BY PROMPT #27

On Mothering & Creating,
On Love & Romance

If tomorrow never came and delivered me this day, our daily bread,
I'd miss never falling in love again
And getting married to the man I adore
(although not in white—I'd wear priestess red or jewel tones like magenta and turquoise or a frock filled with flowers and fringe—like Stevie Nicks, as virginal white has never really been my color).

I'd miss that late summer wedding in a glowing grove of old oak trees,
Strung with amber firefly lights
And dancing under a Harvest Moon.

I'd miss creating a family of my own
Of becoming a mother to beings beyond my friends, my plants, my clients—
Of becoming a mother to my own flesh and blood.

I want to share the joys (and the sacrifices),
Of bringing babies into this world
Of kissing-counting fragile fingers and tiny toes.

Of engaging, in the most radical creative experiment of all:
Creating life in my womb and unleashing those wild little rockstars
and cosmic travelers onto the New Earth,
so I may leave behind a legacy of love in little people.

I'd miss never getting to own that dog Sadie,
who I have seen in my minds' eye for so many years:
The black and white Australian Shepherd,
with the sexy (like her namesake) red bandana around her neck,
and the tan freckles on her paws and her nose.

I'd miss never creating a home with that husband—
to live in the house with the stained-glass window
tucked secretly in the nook of the wrap around staircase.
And tending to the beautiful organic garden all on our own.
A place to blow bubbles and honor the fairies,
To create flower essences and lead workshops.
To offer gifts to the Great Mother,
And to make sweet, sweet love upon the grassy soil.

I'd miss all those quiet moments, strung softly between the BIG BOLD CELEBRATIONS.
I'd miss the hummingbird visits and the butterfly kisses,
the taste of jasmine tea and the sound of rain.
I'd miss sunsets and moonrises and the smell of spring.

(continued)

I'd miss laughing so hard until I almost pee my pants,
Howling, as tears roll down my cheeks.
I'd even miss the times of sadness, signaling growth and the release of pain.

I pray that tomorrow does come and deliver me this day, our daily bread.
I pray the best is yet to come. For there is still so much I want to mother, to create, to love and
To romance.

© *Jana Carrey, April 2020*

My Dream Child

Whatever you may be
Whatever name already is
When I think of you;
The possibility of someone not wanting to be your parent...
Over a silly number.
For to them that is all you are to them. A number.
To me—you are so much more.
"8–12 years olds are most likely to never be adopted until they become legal adults and leave the foster care system"
I don't understand it.
I don't understand that.
No . . . I already know that you will be your own person.
You will have so much of yourself already figured out.
Authentic likes and dislikes
A fully formed little person who just needs their own cheerleader.
Someone on the sidelines; ready and waiting to pick you up and tell you to keep going.
I want to be that and so much more.
I want to see you wildly succeed.
In any manner. Every manner.
Any form. Any way. Any shape or size.
There is a right that must be wronged. Ones that I saw my mother make over and over.
No child should ever feel left feeling like that.
So I eagerly grab my pom-poms.
I give you my loudest cheer.
GIVE ME A N!
GIVE ME AN O!
Because that is what I am saying to anything standing in my way of you.
My child.

© *Peyton Ashby, April 2020*

PROMPT #28

Many of us have a tendency to undervalue ourselves especially when we see other people making so many personal sacrifices. This is especially true during the time of COVID-19, where we are witnessing so many acts of heroism by our healthcare workers. However not all of us are doctors, nurses, or other medical professionals. It also means that the contribution to society by you is not going to be as evident to others.

Think about what you have done to make the world a better place during this pandemic. This is your opportunity to brag judgment free.

When you are ready, please write poetically about what you have done to enhance the lives of others during this health crisis.

POEMS INSPIRED BY PROMPT #28

Applause

Clear the room:
Here comes The Queen.
The Queen of Social D.

I am so distant you can't
see me, taste me, smell me.
I'm six feet in all directions
width, height, depth.

I am shining like a lighthouse.
I beam and the world moves out of my way.
I'm on fire. My eyes, my eys are diamonds
in this treasure chest of isolation.

My kindness is unmatched!
I'm a volunteer go-to for the end-of-the-world gang.
Call me anytime, I say: online, offline, video, audio—
damn, this girl is rocking the phone.

I worship the frontline folks, of course:
The healthcare workers, doctors, nurses,
grocery store, deli, and bodega workers,
the bicycle delivery squad, the UPS, the FedEx,
and all the postal workers.

I clap—for them I clap every night from
my New York window, and when I clap,
the earth shakes and they feel the love
this Queen is sending.

I clap so hard the neighbors roll.
I clap so hard the city rocks.

And you should see me in the morning: quiet,
calm. I meditate so deep I leave a vacuum
in the atmosphere where my ego used to be.
You should see what gets sucked into that hole:
fear, anxiety, boredom, and all those petty words
that could have been.

Why do I do all this? Why do I put that crown
on my head each morning and say, "You got this, girl."

Heh, heh—you know why?
Heh, heh—you know why.

Because I am you—the one who isn't about to quit,
who won't give up in this time of unmatched tragedy.

I am you—the one who comforts fears, who supports
friends and family, neighbors and strangers with
kindness, humor, unlimited love.

I am you—you Queen, you King, you unheralded hero.

I am you, like you—alive.

And oh, how delicious to know that,
here, in just this moment.

© *Kat Georges, April 2020*

Therapy in the Time of Corona

Angst and fear I hear the plea
"I'm all alone please don't forget about me"
I hear you and see you now through a screen
Your eyes tell a tale only this virus has seen.
I try be there as best I can for my patients and their sorrows in a room without
    touch but through Zoom.
I feel their helpless cries and wish I could analyze their innermost woes
But this virus does not have a Freudian or jungian treatment but a traumatic
    moment where we have all froze.
The inner wounds of wearing
Masks and feelings of terror are what my patients ask.
"How do we survive this? When will it end? What kind of a future is in our path?"
My heart swells with love and tenderness as I listen in earnest to their
    deepest quest.

© *Mindi Schumaker-Rivin, April 2020*

POEMS INSPIRED BY PROMPT #28

Wrap Your Troubles in Dreams and Write Your Troubles Away

I like to think that I am making a tiny contribution
To making the world a better place
I know I am making my life a better life to live
COVID-19 has created real heroes
Doctors, nurses, firefighters, cops
Everyday people like truck drivers, teachers, cleaners, cooks
And so many more . . .
My contribution?
Even in isolation, my partner and I can Zoom gather others
Guide them to think about what is amiss
Then help them to gracefully reframe . . .
We ask them to close their eyes and dream . . .
Memories of what's been cherished bubble up
Conjecture about the future looms
But what we have to deal with is THE NOW . . .
We make a verbal snapshot of our own now
We read these poems and stories aloud
Speak and you shall be heard—and healed
Once we can gather again in one room
I feel a literary Tupperware party coming on . . .

© *Barbara Ligeti, April 2020*

About the Contributors

CYNTHIA ADLER is an Actor, Writer, and award winning Socio-Political Satirist. She was one of the top Voice Over actors in America and is an Environmental Activist, now on the Board of Energy Vision, known for its expertise on alternative fuels, research, education programs and outreach.
(Page 12)

JEFFREY ALTSHULER is a Writer, Producer and Director working in Film and Theater. He created *Scenario, the Magazine of Screenwriting Art* and acts as a consultant and advisor on screenwriting projects. He also had an extensive career in TV commercial production. In an earlier life, he was deeply involved in the show horse world and can still muck out a stall, if asked nicely.
(Pages 22, 78, 96)

PEYTON ASHBY is a proud alumnus of Chapman University Class of '15 and is currently pursuing a career in Makeup Artistry. Having found a new vigor with a brand new life, her goal is to make sure others like her never feel alone in the world.
(Pages 113, 137)

JANA CARREY is is a Divine Feminine Mentor, Teacher & Lightworker. She is the Founder of Jana Carrey Healing: "Ancient Alchemy for Modern Beings," which fuses together a unique combination of channeled intuitive guidance, quantum energy healing, flower essence therapy & spiritual counseling. Visit www.janacarrey.com, Instagram & Facebook: @janacarreyhealing.
(Pages 112, 136)

KATE CONNOR is a writer, director and actor. Her award-winning WWII feature *Fort McCoy* which she wrote/directed and starred in with Eric Stoltz, is based on a true story when her family lived next to a Nazi POW camp in Wisconsin. As an actor, Kate has starred in films and TV shows in Europe, Africa and the U.S. Kate has written scripts for Oscar-winning companies. She will next direct a modern film noir based on her adaptation of the novel *Blackmailer* by George Axelrod. Kate, a former attorney, is writing a legal thriller inspired by one of her cases.
(Pages 4, 133)

About the Contributors *(continued)*

BRIAN DELATE, as an actor, has had a colorful and exciting career in film, theatre and television, from Broadway to Europe to Vietnam. He also has been prolific as a writer for screen and stage. "These last years have been a divine convergence of my history as a decorated combat, non-commissioned officer in Vietnam, with my artistry. How fortunate—how purposeful."
(Pages 87, 102)

PHOEBE DIFTLER is a Thai Massage Therapist and a Yoga Instructor, conducting teacher training and workshops across the country. She is the author of *Phoethaiyoga.com: Urban Guide to Ancient Thai Massage*. Phoebe has had a career as a graphic designer and creative director. She was introduced to ShiftPoetry™ by Barbara Ligeti and Howard Kern, who were her students in her Restorative Yoga class. She was thrilled to discover that she could write poetry.
(Pages 16, 61)

STEVE FIFE has had 12 books published, five by Cune Press (Seattle), including two collections of poetry, *Twisted Hipster* and *Dreaming in the Maze of Love-Grief-Madness*. Steve has been the recipient of a Federal Poetry Grant and is the writer-in-residence at the Ark Theatre in North Hollywood. He is thankful to Shift-Poetry™ for getting him back to writing new poems.
(Pages 32, 45, 55)

STEFANIE FLETCHER has been doing humanitarian work for 38 years including nursing and volunteer disaster medical work. She is now in her fourth year of Chinese Medicine school. She is married to her best friend Mark and is a proud mother of two sons and a granddaughter, Ava. She loves her sweet furry and feathered friends too, which include three dogs, four cats, and four lovebirds!
(Pages 50, Page 56)

About the Contributors *(continued)*

ROBERT GALINSKY is a performance and media coach whose clients include 50 Cent (Rapper/Actor), Libby Moore (Oprah Winfrey's Chief of Staff), and Kofi Appenteng (President, Africa-America Institute; Board, Ford Foundation). He works with incarcerated youth in NYC and LA and has served inmates at Rikers Island Jail for the past 6 years. As a writer/performer he debuted Off-Broadway at the Cherry Lane Theatre in his critically acclaimed solo piece "The Bench a Homeless Love Story." The play is having a life in many cities. Robert attracts media for good causes and he has shaped and co-written over fifty TEDx Talks.
(Pages 126, 127, 128)

KAT GEORGES is a New York City-based poet, playwright, performer, publisher, and graphic designer. She has written and staged twelve plays, and is the author of two books: *Our Lady of the Hunger* (poems) and *Three Somebodies: Plays about Notorious Dissidents* (plays). She is co-founder, editor, and artistic director of Three Rooms Press (New York), a fiercely-independent publisher of work inspired by dada, punk, and passion. She lives in Greenwich Village.
(Page 140)

ASEEM GIRI is a wellness entrepreneur with a successful track record starting and exiting companies. He also has a passion for fine art. He is based in Los Angeles.
(Page 44)

CHRISTINA HELENA is a speaker, writer and performer based in New York City. As one of the youngest pancreatic cancer survivors with a thirteen-inch scar across her abdomen, she is redefining and modernizing the stigma behind trauma and pain with one simple thought: "My Scar is Sexy." Christina's story is currently in development as an off-Broadway solo show entitled *SCAR*. Her TEDx talk is about the perceived fear of mortality humans have as a substitution for self-responsibility for resolution of one's pain. Visit www.ChristinaHelena.com
(Page 70)

JEFFREY HOLLANDER has spent most of his professional life as a seasoned Life Insurance Industry Advanced Sales Professional with over 30 years of experience. Before acting as Advanced Sales Lead at MassMutual Insurance Company from 2016-2019, Jeffrey was an Assistance Vice President of Advanced Markets at MetLife, where he worked for 24 years. Retired at the end of 2019, Jeffrey welcomes new challenges in his life, including tapping his creativity and just taking time to smell the roses.
(Pages 9, 28, 99)

HOWARD KERN is a Los Angeles based corporate attorney who writes articles and short stories. He edited his alma mater's Law Review. Howard "wrote himself well" after difficult times in his life and with Barbara Ligeti has "packaged" his bibliotherapeutic technique calling it ShiftPoetry.™ This book grew out of Zoom-delivered ShiftPoetry™ workshops in March/April of 2020. Previously Howard, with Barbara, co-authored and edited *Collected Memories* an anthology of works written by various authors and ShiftPoets in Hydra, Greece, in October, 2018. For more on Howard visit www.ShiftPoetry.com
(Pages vi, 40, 51, 54, 60, 71, 74, 103, 108, 116, 122)

MICHELLE KOZA is a high school English teacher in New York City. All the worthwhile lessons she's learned in her life are a result of this.
(Pages 38, 86)

BARBARA LIGETI After 9/11 in New York City Barbara staged writing and improv workshops for firefighters, policeman, and a range of first responders. Co-creating ShiftPoetry™ with Howard Kern is a logical extension of her dedication to helping folks to understand themselves and others through the arts and through heart based honest self-expression. Visit www.BarbaraLigeti.com.
(Pages 47, 104, 117, 142)

About the Contributors *(continued)*

JENIFER WINTERS O'NEILL has been a publisher, a radio host, and a consultant for various businesses including not-for-profits. Notably, she published "Relevant Times", a website driven magazine and internet radio program focused on sustainable living in the New York Metropolitan area. Her favorite positions in life are as wife to Jim and mother of two boys, James and Ben, and she loves her four-legged family members. Jenifer is so grateful for her experience with Shift Poetry™. She says "It has been both healing and empowering—especially in this most challenging time for the world. Thank you Howard and Barbara for the opportunity to share my words."
(Pages 64, 75, 120)

PAT PATTERSON is an accomplished actor and producer. She has found her way onstage Off Broadway and on Theatre Row in LA. She loves film and has produced features and shorts. Presently she is working on a TV Pilot *Hereafter Here* which explores what happens when we die. She values the spoken and written word and is pleased to be included in this anthology.
(Pages 5, 13, 34)

JESSE PUDLES is an actor, Open Temple teacher, and now trainer for a remote team of COVID-19 Relief in New York City. He has been gifted with the opportunity to use others' words to impart important stories and truths about the world to students and audiences across the United States. With the help of Shift-Poetry™ and in this book, Jesse, a Millennial, is finally sharing his own words about who he is and what he wants in this time of uncertainty.
(Page 8, 92, 132)

MICHELLE SCHRUPP loves travel and living life to the fullest with her best friend & husband Brad. She was delighted to meet Howard and Barbara in Vietnam at the onset of ShiftPoetry™, and feels joy in supporting their work in getting others to write themselves healthy.
(Page 23)

About the Contributors *(continued)*

MARK SCHULTE is an actor and writer from St. Cloud, Minnesota, who lives on the UWS of Manhattan with his wife and children. In addition to writing and performing, he teaches theatre at a high needs NYC Public High School.
(Pages 18, 29, 79, 82, 93)

MINDI SCHUMAKER-RIVIN has been a psychotherapist in private practice for over 25 years in LA working with individuals and couples struggling with life. She also specializes in working with Creative Blocks and trauma. She says "I love helping people find their true voice." She has been called a "zen psychoanalyst."
(Page 141)

CHAS TIMBERLAKE is a ship-owner and frustrated renaissance man, juggling 24/7 commitments with a love of fine arts, theater, and poetry. COVID-19 has afforded him time to reconnect with the important things in life, viz. his family, writing, music, and what the world can look like if we take the time and energy to make it happen.
(Page 129)

RUTH WAYTZ has degrees in English and Advertising and has earned a living through writing and editing (one way or another) since the 1980s. She won an Emmy for her work on *Jeopardy!* and has supervised dozens of books for a major ghostwriting agency. She has her own publishing imprint and coaches writers through the publishing process. Ruth's expertise crosses many fields: tech, automotive, legal, comedy, esoterica, and the arts. She has a broad range of clients. She calls editing, "what you meant to say, not what you said."
(Pages 41, 67)

DEBORAH WILLIAMS is happily retired after many years in public service. When not quarantined, she spends her days helping to care for three beautiful grandchildren, learning to play piano and other new hobbies. She loves her family and friends with abandon and is generally in an excellent mood.
(Pages 26, 65, 90, 97)

Acknowledgements

Thank you to all of our ShiftPoets for writing with open hearts, a sense of adventure, without judgement and for being perfect—as we all are "perfectly imperfect"

Extra thanks to Jeffrey Altshuler for his editorial support and to Ruth Waytz for her second set of eyes.

Special thanks to Kat Georges for her creativity, keen eye, constant support and openness to share her vast experience

—Howard and Barbara

About ShiftPoetry™

Barbara Ligeti and Howard Kern are the co-creators of ShiftPoetry.™

Barbara has had a long career in many aspects of media—from on-camera talent to producing, writing and directing. As a wellness expert, her toolbox includes extensive training and credentials in meditation, coaching, yoga, pilates, movement therapy, nutrition, and other modalities. Notably she ran theatrical writing workshops and expressive healing circles in New York City post 9/11.

Howard Kern is a corporate attorney and as a student was an editor of his alma mater's law review. He is a coach. He has won prizes for his short stories. He has used the process of writing intuitively to better his life—in particular, to heal from severe losses and his personal health issues. When he got together with Barbara his desire was to share his bibliotherapeutic technique with other people in all walks.

Howard's devotion to practice and Barbara's skill at positioning and shaping came together to birth ShiftPoetry™ a fresh, thriving, innovative way to better lives.

During difficult times ShiftPoetry™ can be easily practiced using existing media, such as Zoom conferencing and YouTube. Because it is all about engaging in words, it is easily accessible through this book.

www.ingramcontent.com/pod-product-compliance
Lightning Source LLC
Chambersburg PA
CBHW020416080526
44584CB00014B/1356